the HIKING and CAMPING GUIDE to the FLAT TOPS WILDERNESS

T0119132

AL MARLOWE and
KAREN CHRISTOPHERSON

WESTWINDS
PRESS®

THE PRUETT SERIES

Library of Congress Cataloging-in-Publication Data
Marlowe, Al, 1938-
  The hiking and camping guide to Colorado's Flat Tops Wilderness /
Al Marlowe and Karen Christopherson. — [Revised edition].
    pages cm
  Original edition published under title: A Hiking and Camping Guide to
the Flat Tops Wilderness Area. Boulder, Colorado : Pruett Publishing, 1994.
  Includes index.
  ISBN 978-0-87108-311-1 (pbk.)
  1. Hiking—Colorado—Flat Tops Wilderness—Guidebooks. 2. Camp-
ing—
Colorado—Flat Tops Wilderness—Guidebooks. 3. Flat Tops Wilderness
(Colo.)—Guidebooks. I. Christopherson, Karen. II. Title.
  GV199.42.C62F555 2014
  796.5109788—dc23
                              2014004310

Author photo, page 226, by Jack Olson Photography.
Area Map on page 6-7 by the State of Colorado.
All trail maps by US Bureau of Land Management.

Design by Vicki Knapton

Published by WestWinds Press®
An imprint of

GRAPHIC ARTS
BOOKS®

P.O. Box 56118
Portland, Oregon 97238-6118
503-254-5591
www.graphicartsbooks.com

*To Arthur Carhart, whose vision was to preserve
the area around Trappers Lake rather than subdivide
the lakeshore for summer cabins, leading to the
Wilderness Act of 1964.*

Contents

Area Map 6
East Trails Map 8
West Trails Map 9

1. The Flat Tops 11
2. Regulations and Common Sense 27
3. Maps for the Flat Tops 40
4. Rio Blanco County Road 8 45
5. North Fork of the White River *(County Roads 8 and 12)* 77
6. Forest Road 205 *(Trappers Lake Road)* 100
7. Forest Road 8 *(County Road 8)* 137
8. Forest Road 16 142
9. State Highway 131 156
10. Eagle County Road 301 179
11. Eagle County Road 301 *(Colorado River Road)* 196
12. Forest Road 600 204

Wilderness Lodges and Outfitters 215
Additional Resources 216
Federal Agencies 217
Emergency Services 218
Index 220
About the Authors 228

Area Map

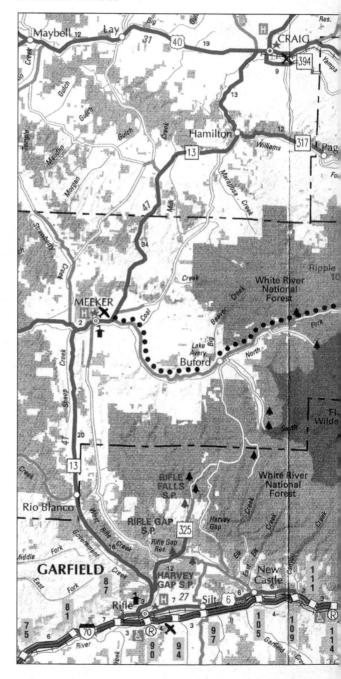

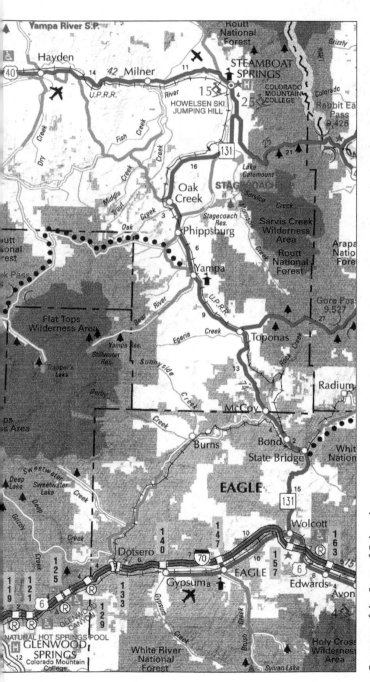

Courtesy of the State of Colorado

7

EAST TRAILS

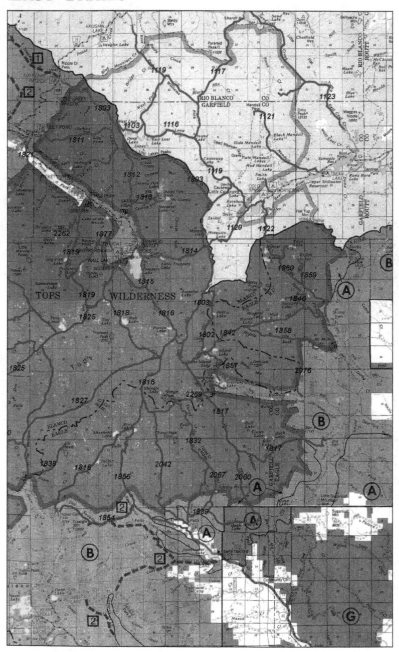

Courtesy of the US Forest Service

8

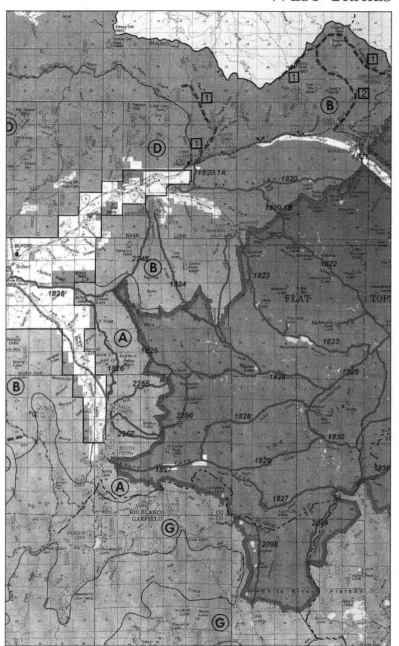

1

THE FLAT TOPS

The Flat Tops Wilderness Area, located in west-central Colorado, is about 150 miles west of Denver, about 100 miles east of Grand Junction, and about 60 miles south from Craig. It is a popular destination for both residents and out-of-state visitors, bounded by Interstate 70 on the south, State Highway 13 on the west, Rio Blanco County Road 8 on the north, and State Highway 131 on the east. It is 267 square miles spread across four counties: Eagle, Garfield, Rio Blanco, and Routt. The boundaries fall within two national forests: White River and Routt. Several hundred miles of trails give hikers access to the area.

The wilderness is unique. It compares with no other mountain range in the state. Only the Columbia Plateau of the Pacific Northwest is similar. There are no tall spires, no fourteeners, found in the

Flat Top Mountain is the highest point in the wilderness at 12,354 feet.

Flat Tops. Rather, it is a massive block of rock pushed upward and planed level, its surface punctured here and there by peaks rising a thousand feet above the high plateau.

The land doesn't test you the way other mountain ranges will. There are few steep-sided peaks. At an average elevation near 11,000 feet, it doesn't starve you of oxygen as climbing a fourteener would. Still, the second largest wilderness in the state offers challenges. A visitor could spend a season and not hike every path. From a distance, the Flat Tops Wilderness lives up to its name. Traveling along State Highway 131, between the communities of Toponas and Yampa, you view the plateau to the west, appearing nearly flat. Here and there, incisions were made in the massive block, formed by stresses deep within the earth during the formation of the Rocky Mountains. Rivers and creeks that drain the land enlarged and deepened the cuts.

Along the west flank of the White River Uplift, the geologic name for the Flat Tops, sedimentary rocks have been folded. Solid rock and overlying sediments deposited by ancient seas were pushed upward by forces of plate tectonics. The sediments conformed to the core rocks in the same way a bedspread drapes a bed. At the edges, the rocks were folded. At a rate imperceptible in a single lifetime, the exposed sediments eroded, and then were swept away by wind and rain, leaving only remnants of folds along the west flank of the Flat Tops. You will find this uplifted, folded, and eroded structure, known as the Grand Hogback between State Highways 13 and 325 near Rifle Gap Reservoir north of Rifle. Along Interstate 70 between Glenwood Springs and New Castle, red sediments sloping steeply to the south give additional testimony to the forces that built the Flat Tops.

The Forest Service estimates that more than 170,000 visitors come to the Flat Tops each year to enjoy the wilderness. They come in all seasons for a variety of reasons. Some visit the excellent mountain lodges. Many come for the fishing and hunting. Backpackers and horsemen travel the trails in the backcountry. And while the number of visitors seems large, as in many places in the backcountry, if you get any distance from edges and trailheads, you encounter fewer people, allowing each individual or group the privacy desired.

History

The written record of the Flat Tops is sparse. Early Spanish explorers traveled the southern and western areas of the state. The Pike Expedition (1806-7) and Long Expedition (1819) explored east of the Rockies. The Western emigration that began following the exploration of the Louisiana Territory took several routes, all of which passed either north or south of the Flat Tops. Very little if any record exists of early American or European explorers venturing into the area other than a few fur trappers.

It is thought by some that humans first used the area about ten thousand years ago. Ute Indians were the most recent Native Americans to inhabit the Flat Tops. For more than two centuries, they traveled and hunted from southern Wyoming to as far south as Taos, New Mexico. Having acquired horses by 1740, they could easily have ventured into the plateau to hunt.

Whites settled the region in the mid-nineteenth century. In 1878, Nathan Meeker was appointed agent for the White River Agency, located near the town that bears his name. His ambitious but ill-advised plan to reform the Ute Indians, changing them into farmers rather than hunters, ended in disaster. Chief Douglas and 25 to 30 Utes set fire to the agency on the White River on September 29, 1879, killing Meeker and 10 other men. Major Thomas T. Thornburgh brought a small force of 153 soldiers from Fort Steele, Wyoming, too late to protect the agency. Near Milk Creek, northeast of town, Chief Colorow and nearly 400 Ute Indians ambushed the force, killing Thornburgh and 12 soldiers. Even though the Indians won the battle, they lost the war when the Army moved them to a reservation in Utah three years later.

Just as a historian pores through old writings, putting together a story, the geologist studies the record of the Flat Tops in the rock. The story tells of the history; how this area came into existence, what makes it unique. It begins nearly three billion years ago.

Viewing the Flat Tops, one could easily believe it is a permanent fixture on the land. Yet, a close look reveals countless streams, draining countless hillsides. Each of these creeks removes tiny particles of rock, eroded by constant weathering. Before our eyes, the mountains that appear so solid are destroyed a grain of sand at a time. This process of building mountain ranges and reducing them to rubble has occurred several times in this area.

The same events that have created the Earth's present form were also at work in molding and sculpting the Flat Tops. Scientists have long speculated that the continents we now know were once united in a single landmass called Pangea. This single, massive continent began to break apart by a process called plate tectonics.

As the single, massive continent began to dissociate, the sea moved into the rifts created. Several times, warm seas covered the lowlands east of the Flat Tops as Pangea crumbled.

The theory of plate tectonics suggests that continents, or plates, not only "drift" around over the Earth's surface, moving apart, they also collide. When two plates crash together, the result is similar to that of two cars bumping—that is, if the collision takes place over eons rather than milliseconds. Fenders bend—sheet metal tears. Land compresses—rock shears.

Continents pushing against each other create tremendous stresses in the land. Compression forces build mountains in a similar way a child might squeeze toy blocks together. The resulting forces fracture solid rock. Continued pressure moves some blocks of rock upward, some are shoved down.

Once blocks of rock are lifted, perhaps several thousand feet above sea level, nature goes to work tearing them down. Freezing and thawing cycles break apart solid rock. Rain and snowmelt remove eroded bits and pieces. Wind scatters small particles of sand. Over hundreds of millennia, once-high mountains are worn into nonexistence. Eroded sediment eventually comes to rest on the ocean floor. Mountains have risen and fallen several times in the Flat Tops region.

Another phenomenon controlled by plate tectonics is volcanism. Oceanic plates are denser than continental plates. On colliding, one oceanic plate moves beneath the other. The denser rock moves deeper, contacting a zone of intense heat, melting the rock. As in a pot of boiling water, bubbles move from the bottom at the heat source, the molten rock boils up, seeking escape. As it rises, continental crust is fractured, creating a path for the liquid magma to spew out and cover the land.

Eruptions away from the plate edges are usually mild, not violent as was Mount St. Helens. Basalt, a thick, black, molten rock coming from deep within the Earth, flows and spreads out over the land in the same way chocolate frosting covers a layer cake. Mount Kilauea in Hawaii, while located on an ocean plate rather than a continent, is such a volcano. The volcanoes of the Flat Tops were similar in activity to Kilauea.

In the past twelve million years, ten or more mild eruptions spread basalt over the plateau. After spreading out over the surface, the basalt cooled, giving the Flat Tops its tabletop appearance. Deep

This U-shaped valley gives evidence of the glaciers that formed drainages in the Flat Tops.

Lake, in the southeast quadrant of the area, was once a volcano on the Flat Tops.

Glaciers have also had a part in sculpting the area. During the most recent Ice Age, ending about ten thousand years ago, they worked on the many fractures in the uplift. Gorges were deepened. Deep Creek and the South Fork of the White River had their streambeds carved by glacial action. The thick sheet of ice carved the Chinese Wall near Trappers Lake.

Rubble was pushed ahead of the advancing ice wall. As the climate warmed and the glaciers melted, ridges of rock left behind formed dams creating lakes here and there. Glaciers dammed Trappers Lake more than once.

The Ice Age ended as the Earth's climate began to warm. Volcanoes no longer pour out smoke and lava. The region has experienced geologic activity, however, over the past ten millennia. Near the town of McCoy, an eruption occurred eight thousand years ago. Just over four thousand years ago, about a mile north of Dotsero, the most recent volcanic eruption in Colorado occurred. The resulting lava flow dammed the Eagle River, creating a shallow lake. Through the ensuing centuries, the river slowly eroded the basalt barrier. The only remaining evidence of the pond you will find is the scattering of black boulders between Interstate 70 and the river, rock that once formed the low dam.

The forces that built the Flat Tops also created an ideal environment for life. The waters contain an abundance of life-sustaining minerals for fish. The vegetation is rich in calcium, enabling elk to grow massive antlers. The land supports the largest deer and elk herds in the state. Wildflowers are abundant, both in quantity and variety.

While the construction of the Flat Tops has ended for now, the area does not remain static. Nature acts continuously, remodeling and then destroying what she has built. It's kind of like the highway construction projects that are always ongoing. A look at the Colorado River in Glenwood Canyon confirms what we know. The river is never clear. It appears as chocolate milk each spring or after a summer thunderstorm, evidence that Nature constantly erodes the land the river drains even as we watch.

The processes that gave us the Flat Tops and the Colorado Rockies also left valuable minerals in the state. Gold deposited by hydrothermal solution in numerous locations throughout the state attracted prospectors to Colorado hoping to strike it rich. The yellow metal, along with silver, molybdenum, and other minerals have contributed to Colorado's economy for more than a century. Several companies mine coal along the Yampa River drainage, east and north of the Flat Tops. With the exception of a small number of oil wells and minor placer gold deposits, the Flat Tops is nearly devoid of economic minerals.

With few resources to exploit, the area remained pristine. Few roads ever penetrated the wilderness on the Flat Tops. The sides are too steep. A short snow-free period of just four or five months and the high altitude make ranching impractical other than summer grazing.

This high plateau has long been recognized as a place worth preserving. Old US Forest Service maps show it as a primitive area. The Trappers Lake area narrowly avoided development early in the twentieth century though. Arthur H. Carhart, a landscape architect working for the Forest Service, convinced his supervisor, Carl J. Stahl, that the lakeshore should be preserved rather than developed for summer home sites. Carhart's dream later became a model for wilderness legislation. After years of debate, Congress passed the Wilderness Act of 1964. President Johnson signed it into law, preserving the Flat Tops. In 1978, Congress enlarged the boundaries, expanding the wilderness to its present size.

In the four thousand years since the eruption at Dotsero Crater, little appears changed in the Flat Tops. A wilderness visitor today will enjoy the same magnificent vistas the Ute Indians saw while hunting in the area a century and more ago. Elk still roam, sending their resonant mating calls echoing across the high glacial valleys each fall. Colorado River cutthroat, though threatened, still swim in their ancestral waters.

Flora and Fauna

Colorado's largest **deer** and **elk** herds live in the area. Because of large herds the Flat Tops is a popular hunting area. Hunter success rates on deer range from 20 to 60 percent, depending on the season and game unit. Elk hunters average from 10 to 40 percent success. Every year, a few lucky hunters take trophy bulls in the wilderness.

While deer and elk are the most common big game, they're not the only large animals that are found in the Flat Tops. Though not

The White River deer herd is the largest in Colorado.

common, bighorn sheep live here. Bear and mountain lion also live in the wilderness. Because both are shy, you're not likely to see either.

Coyotes are as widespread here as in other places in the West. You'll hear them serenading the moon most often at evening or dawn. The coyote's song makes a wilderness trip complete.

The Flat Tops is home for many small animals. You'll find **cottontail rabbits** and **snowshoe hares**. **Porcupines** are likely to appear anywhere. **Chipmunks** may invade your camp. And **pine squirrels** will disturb the peace with their annoying, mindless chatter in the pine and spruce forests. Field mice will be attracted to any tasty morsels you may have in your camp. These tiny tan creatures are most active after dark, when they feel safe from predators. Another small critter you find—you're more likely to hear it rather than see it at first—resembles a mouse. You'll occasionally catch a glimpse of a **vole** run-

Moose were transplanted into the state beginning in the 1970s. They are seen frequently in the wilderness.

ning through tunnels in the grass and leaves. They're darker than mice and have very short tails.

The many high lakes and ponds are attractive to two furbearers: **beaver** and **muskrat**. Beaver become active at dusk as they begin swimming about the ponds. After dark, they work hard—well, they're busy as beavers—downing aspens to build and repair dams. Muskrats are much more casual about life. You may find these small, gray rodents at any time of day.

Birds are found on the Flat Tops in abundance. Songbirds include **robins**, **chickadees**, **Steller's** and **gray jays**, and **warblers**. Occasionally, you'll hear the deep croak of a passing **raven**. **Woodpeckers** include hairy and downy, as well as flickers. Should you plan your visit in one of the many campgrounds, you may want to take a hummingbird feeder. Two species, the broadtail and Rufus, will be attracted to the nectar.

Red-tailed hawks are one of the more common birds of prey you'll see on the Flat Tops. With a bit of luck, you may see a peregrine falcon. You may also spot a golden eagle soaring high above the plateau, using its incredible vision to sight a tiny meal.

Waterfowl find the area attractive. **Mallards** and **teal** use beaver ponds to raise families. Another game bird found on the Flat Tops is the **dusky (blue) grouse**. You'll run across these birds on the edges, openings close to timber. **Wild turkey** have been successfully introduced in the region and do well wherever they find feed in winter. Moose have also found the Flat Tops favorable in the past twenty years, the result of introduction by Colorado Parks and Wildlife (CPW).

The Flat Tops is an area having large open meadows and immense stands of dense timber. The most common trees are spruce, fir, and lodgepole pines. You will observe large numbers of snags—standing dead trees—in the wilderness. Back in the 1940s and '50s, an invasion of spruce beetles killed many trees. Even after nearly fifty years, many are still standing. They're also a potential hazard in high wind.

Flat Tops visitors may question the reason for so many dead standing trees in the wilderness. As with all living things forests have finite lives. The life span of a forest may be measured in centuries, even millennia rather than years. A forester with the Colorado State Forest Service informed us that a healthy forest should have 60 to 150 trees per acre. As the number increases, trees compete for nutrients from the soil and for sunlight. Trees that are stressed become susceptible to disease, which leads to infestation of tree-killing insects such as pine and ips beetles. Unless a beetle-killing freeze occurs, they will survive to lay eggs on other nearby trees.

Unhealthy and dead trees are also susceptible to fire, whether caused by lightning or by a careless visitor. Several major fires have occurred in the Flat Tops in the past few decades. In 1979 the lower Derby Creek drainage burned. The Ute Creek fire of 1993 destroyed many acres of trees near the head of the creek on the northwest side of the wilderness. Lightning strikes caused fires in 2002 that burned the west slopes along the North Fork of the White, spreading to the Big Fish Lake area, and Trappers Lake. A second fire burned the Lost Lakes area south of Ripple Creek Pass. We can't do anything about naturally caused fires but visitors can exercise caution with cooking and campfires.

Aspen groves are scattered all over the Flat Tops, especially at the lower elevations. They are a special attraction in the fall. Then, entire slopes will appear as a solid yellow or gold. Along streams and lakes, willows grow profusely. Sage also is found, usually on low elevation slopes.

Because of plentiful moisture, grasses are lush on the Flat Tops. Interspersed in the grasses is a multitude of wildflowers. Hidden among openings in the aspens, you'll find columbines, the state flower.

Color varies with the season. July brings a variety of species and colors. Red, pink, white, blue, and yellow flowers often appear as a multicolored shag carpet. Blue flax, red elephants, lupines, and countless others decorate the wilderness. Fireweed's pink blossoms spring up along cuts and bare areas. Paintbrush adds reds to plain green weed patches in small openings in the timber. By August, yellows predominate. Daisies, sunflowers, and even dandelions color the hillsides. Whatever the season, throughout the summer, you'll find a variety of colors.

Climate

Because of its location, the Flat Tops receives an abundance of precipitation, making the region an angler's paradise. The plateau is the first obstacle any eastward-moving weather system encounters in this part of the state. The topography creates its own weather. Prevailing winds are from the west. Air moving from the west is forced to ascend to cross the wilderness, cooling in the process. Cooling condenses the water vapor, producing clouds that soon reach their dew point, bringing precipitation. This is a frequent year-round occurrence on the Flat Tops.

Winter snowfalls are abundant. Often, by early November, the plateau is inaccessible. The mantle of white rarely recedes before the following summer, in June or even July.

Summer afternoon thundershowers are common. The day may begin with clear skies but by noon, the first clouds form. Moments later, lightning flashes and thunder resounds across the plateau. The shower that follows may be brief but intense or it can be a prelude to several days of rain. Be aware, though, that snow can fall at any time of year, even in summer.

While the region does receive more than its fair share of precipitation, summer also brings pleasant warm, dry periods. Even at 11,000 feet, the days can be hot. Daytime temperatures range from the 40s or 50s to the 80s. Lows can vary from below freezing to the 50s.

Big game hunting seasons begin with archery in late August and extend through November. Though August and September are still summer on the calendar, the prudent hunter will prepare for the extremes. The first significant snow may fall in September, though it usually melts off in a few days. Jack Frost makes his first appearance then, too, bringing the first fall color to the high country.

October frequently delivers a lull in weather patterns. Deer and elk hunters often find the day balmy in spite of nighttime freezes. It's still wise to prepare for severe conditions, though. Late in the month, the season has progressed enough that snow begins accumulating. Shorter days and cooler temperatures mean less melting.

Soon, the plateau will be covered in white, inaccessible until the following summer.

The wilderness is closed half the year to all but snowshoers and cross-country skiers. And while high lakes begin to open in May, most trails are still drifted shut. A trip to one of the early opening lakes requires skis or snowshoes. As a general guideline, areas below 9,000 feet are usually accessible by Memorial Day. In June, plan your trips to locations below 10,000 feet and by July, the entire wilderness should be open though you may find scattered snowdrifts. Of course, all this is dependent on the winter snowfall and exposure. South facing areas tend to open first. In dry years, the wilderness may open earlier.

Access

The Flat Tops Wilderness is accessed from four highways: Interstate 70 on the south, State Highway 13 on the west, US Highway 40 on the north, and State Highway 131 on the east. From these roads, the towns of Steamboat Springs, Craig, Meeker, Rifle, New Castle, Glenwood Springs, Dotsero, Yampa, Phippsburg, and Oak Creek offer access to the wilderness.

Interstate 70 runs east–west across Colorado. It is the primary access route to the Flat Tops from Denver, east of the Rockies, and from Grand Junction to the west, 30 miles from the Utah line. The road follows the Colorado River along the south side of the White River Plateau.

From the town of Rifle, go north on State Highway 13 from Interstate 70. This two-lane, paved road takes you along the Grand Hogback on the west flank of the plateau to the town of Meeker, 41 miles from Rifle. Meeker is a good place to fill your gas tank, buy groceries, or a fishing/hunting license before venturing to the wilderness.

US Highway 40, while it doesn't traverse the plateau, does give access to the wilderness from the north. Craig is 48 miles north of Meeker. On the west side of Craig, State Highway 13 goes south to Meeker from US 40.

From Steamboat Springs, 42 miles east of Craig on US 40 and at the west side of Rabbit Ears Pass, State Highway 131 goes south to join Interstate 70 at Wolcott. State Highway 131 passes through the communities of Oak Creek, Phippsburg, and Yampa, each of which gives access to the eastern areas of the wilderness.

Kremmling, a small ranching community, lies 52 miles southeast of Steamboat Springs and 112 miles west of Denver, also on US 40. It doesn't give access to the Flat Tops, but 6 miles west of town, take State Highway 134 over Gore Pass to connect with State Highway 131. Yampa is 9 miles north of the 131/134 junction.

In addition to the major state and federal all-weather roads, there is a network of county roads accessing the wilderness. From New Castle, 11 miles west of Glenwood Springs on Interstate 70, a gravel road, the New Castle–Buford Road, takes you north to Buford. In the White River National Forest, it's Forest Road 244 and in Rio Blanco County, its designation is County Road 17.

Rio Blanco County Road 8 heads east from Meeker and gets you into the north side of the wilderness. Between Meeker and the Lost Creek Guard Station east of Buford, the road is paved for a distance of about 25 miles. At the forest boundary, the road is well-maintained gravel. The road takes you over Ripple Creek Pass and on to the towns of Oak Creek, Phippsburg, and Yampa, another 40 miles east. From Yampa, Routt County Road 7 on the south side of town leads west for 17 miles to Stillwater Reservoir over narrow, rough pavement, which changes to gravel at the forest boundary.

Eagle County Road 301, also named the Colorado River Road, is a good gravel road that follows the Colorado River. It takes off from State Highway 131 near the community of McCoy. This road provides wilderness access from Derby, Sweetwater, and Deep Creek Roads.

Forest Road 600 leaves Eagle County Road 301 at the Colorado River, 1.5 miles north of Interstate 70. This road is the only access to the south side of the wilderness, 39 miles from the blacktop.

Road access is dependent both on maintenance and season. Federal and state highways are maintained in all weather conditions. County roads are cleared where year-round access is needed. Roads that are usually, but not always, opened by Memorial Day are Rio Blanco County Road 8 over Ripple Creek Pass, Routt County Road 7 to Stillwater Reservoir, and Garfield County Road 150 up Sweetwater Creek. Forest Road 600, on the plateau leading to the southeast part of the wilderness, is usually open by July 4, sometimes earlier. It's best to check with the White River National Forest supervisor at Glenwood Springs, (970) 319-2670, before making travel plans.

2

REGULATIONS AND COMMON SENSE

Along with the freedom to travel wherever you like, there's a responsibility. Most of us care about a quality wilderness experience. It's the few who don't care that make regulations necessary. Fortunately, most are commonsense practices that will make your Flat Tops visit more enjoyable. Flat Tops Wilderness regulations are available from Forest Service offices in Glenwood Springs, Eagle, Rifle, Meeker, and Yampa, and are posted at all trailheads.

▶ Locate campsites, campfires, and recreational stock at least 100 feet from lakes, streams, and trails. At Hooper, Keener, Trappers, and Smith Lakes, locate camps a quarter mile from the lakeshore. Camping is allowed only in designated sites at Deer Lake. Vegetation and soils adjacent to lakes and streams are sensitive to disturbance. Camping away from trails and lakes adds to a visitor's sense of solitude.

▶ The largest party size is a combination of 25 people and/or recreational stock. Larger groups require a permit because they tend to damage trails and campsites.

▶ Use of motorized vehicles, motorized equipment, motorboats, or other forms of mechanical transport such as bicycle, handcarts, etc., within the wilderness is prohibited.

▶ Landing of aircraft or dropping of materials, supplies, or persons from aircraft in the wilderness is prohibited.

▶ Camping, campfires, and hitching or tethering of recreational stock is prohibited within a quarter mile of Trappers Lake.

▶ Dogs, except for working stock dogs and those used for legal hunting purposes, will be on a leash not to exceed 6 feet in length when within a quarter mile of Trappers Lake. Pets must be under control at all times. Uncontrolled dogs should not be permitted to harass wildlife and other visitors.

▶ For livestock, bring in only processed feeds or pellets. Only certified weed-free hay is permitted in national forests, wilderness areas, and state lands. Pack animals are a part of the wilderness experience for some visitors. Hikers and backpackers meeting riders and pack animals should step off the trail until they pass. If you take Phydeaux, restrain him until horses have passed to avoid spooking them.

▶ Equipment, personal property, or supplies may not be left for more than fourteen continuous days.

▶ Wash at least 100 feet from lakes and streams. Use biodegradable soap and dispose of waste water in the soil. This is to prevent contaminating the water.

▶ Bury human waste at least 100 feet from lakes and streams and 6 inches in the soil so it will decompose naturally.

▶ Pack out everything you bring in and any other trash you may find along the way. Food scraps and bits of paper may be burned. Do not bury trash or food scraps.

▶ Avoid fragile areas. Do not shortcut trails on switchbacks, especially in places others will follow and create new paths that lead to erosion. Rarely will the practice save time.

▶ You are requested to register at wilderness trailheads to assist USFS personnel in managing the wilderness. It also helps rangers locate you in case of emergency. Lodges and outfitters are required to have permits and usually have small areas reserved for their use for campsites. Only the outfitters, their employees, and clients may use these areas. These sites are identified by a

Fireweed are found almost everywhere in the Flat Tops. They were given their name for being one of the first plants to appear following a fire.

Forest Service permit near the camp. When using a guide or outfitter, clients are advised to verify that these businesses have the proper permits.

▶ There's no need to dig a trench around any modern, well-made backpacking tent. It's also unsightly and leads to erosion of the volcanic clay soils that predominate here.

▶ In some cases, the use of wheelchairs by the disabled may be permitted. Check with the Forest Service first, though.

▶ No matter where we go, trash will always be found. There is no excuse for leaving litter. Most camping garbage can be burned. Aluminum beverage cans should be crushed, and then packed out. After all, they weighed almost a pound when you took them in full and almost nothing when you take them out empty.

▶ While they may not be trash, meat poles put up by hunters detract from the visual experience in the wilderness. If you need one, build it using rope rather than bailing wire, which cuts into trees, then dismantle it when you pack out your game. Fluorescent flagging to mark downed game is also unsightly. If you must use flagging, remove it when it's no longer needed. Many hunters use horses in the Flat Tops. Rather than build corrals using logs, nails, and wire to contain stock, it's better to use rope.

The most important rule to remember in the wilderness is to respect the land. Practicing low impact travel preserves the land for future generations. Treat the Flat Tops as if you owned it. The wilderness is *your* land. Respect it.

The Flat Tops has a lot of snags caused by disease and insects years ago. For this reason, be especially careful with fires, whether using wood or a stove. Keep your campfire small. Use only dead wood. Also, select a campsite away from snags. The USFS estimates that 10 snags per acre are felled by wind each year.

Douse your fire anytime you leave camp. Should your unattended fire spread, you can be held financially responsible for the expense of fighting it.

After you break camp, scatter the rocks from your fire ring. Cover the ashes with debris. Better yet, dig a small pit for your fire, saving the sod. When you leave, replace the sod. Use brush to "sweep" the area you tracked with your lug-soled boots. Do the same to trampled vegetation. In a short time, your campsite will appear to have never been used.

Wild Animals

While bears, lions, coyotes, and other carnivores live in the Flat Tops, you're unlikely to have problems with any of them. Chipmunks that steal your GORP and gray jays that beg handouts are normally the extent of predation experienced by visitors. That doesn't mean you shouldn't use caution.

Bears are the most feared because of their size, their teeth and claws, and the fact that they eat whatever they want. Most will try to avoid you. Since bears are always hungry, food smells can attract them. The use of commercial freeze-dried foods kept in original packages will reduce the odor problem.

Don't eat or store food in your tent. Burn trash and food scraps. Keep your campsite clean.

If you see a bear on the trail, make noise. Don't approach it. If the animal comes toward you, don't turn and run. Instead, slowly back away until you are in a safer position. Try to get upwind so the bear can catch your scent. Should you carry bear repellent, that is, a .357 or .500 S&W Magnum? Chances are you'll never need a gun for protection from bears or other wild animals in the wilderness.

Should you see a mountain lion, consider yourself lucky. In four decades of living in and traveling the backcountry, the closest I have come to a big cat is finding tracks.

So, if you should be so fortunate, how do you react? First of all, don't run. This will induce a cat to attack. Face the animal but avoid eye contact, which the cat perceives as a threat. Raise your arms to appear larger. Speak softly to the animal and begin backing away.

Colorado Parks and Wildlife publishes several free pamphlets concerning dangerous animals. One thing CPW doesn't state is that a person may use whatever effective means to stop a genuine life-endangering threat.

Other carnivores you'll possibly see in the Flat Tops pose little threat. Bobcats are secretive. They're usually seen only when running away. Coyotes normally avoid humans.

Hypothermia

No matter what season you visit the Flat Tops, hypothermia is possible. In winter, the obvious contributor is cold and snow. The hazard also exists in summer.

Because the Flat Tops gets rain frequently, and the high elevation causes lower temperatures, you should stay dry. Modern rain gear makes this possible.

The problem is not just the dampness but also the chill it produces. Relative humidity at high elevations is usually low, causing rapid evaporation. An air temperature of 50°F, combined with a 10 mph wind, can give the same cooling effect as a temperature in the 40s. If a sudden shower has soaked your clothes, the evaporation causes even more cooling. Most cases of hypothermia occur at temperatures between 30°F and 50°F.

Hypothermia will cause severe shivering, slurred speech, incoherence, stumbling, drowsiness, and extreme fatigue. If you do get wet and notice any of the symptoms in yourself or someone with you, immediate treatment is advised. Get out of the wind. Remove all wet clothes. Put on dry clothes and crawl into a sleeping bag. The victim should be given warm drinks if coherent and able to swallow. It may be necessary to use your own body heat to warm a hypothermic person.

Lightning

Thunderstorms occur frequently in the Flat Tops. So does lightning. The plateau has several large clear areas, free of trees. Be cautious about hiking in the open anytime storms are threatening. If electrical storms are a possibility, stay close to shelter. During an electrical storm, avoid open areas or lone trees.

If you are caught in the open, remove your pack, which likely contains conductive metal. Squat down with your feet apart. Form a ball with your body. In this position, a lightning strike should pass over your body in what's called a flashover. Keeping your feet together is like closing a switch. It completes the electrical circuit. Only in this case, you are the circuit.

Forest Fire

Get out of the area and don't hang around to watch it. Report fires to the nearest USFS district office.

This photo, taken a year after the Big Fish Fire, shows ground cover recovering. Fireweed, one of the first plants to return following a burn, is scattered among the burned trees.

Other Hazards

The Flat Tops has lots of standing dead trees. Select a campsite with this in mind. Strong winds, common in the Flat Tops, are all it takes to knock one down.

Get your water only from known safe sources or treat it before drinking. Assume that any surface water is contaminated. Water can be filtered, boiled, or chemically treated to kill giardia. Using only water that has been processed with barley and hops will also eliminate such problems. Oh. While a beer may taste good after hiking all day, be aware that alcohol can also contribute to dehydration, a cause of altitude illness.

Insects are abundant on the Flat Tops. Bring repellent. Lots. Garlic is also said to repel mosquitoes. It's effective also in capsule form. This is available from your pharmacy or health food store.

Snakes are not a serious problem. Most of those you see are garter snakes. You might even come across an occasional bull snake. They're harmless. The worst that would come of a bite is tetanus and almost everyone has been immunized against that. Should a bite become infected an antibiotic may be needed. Timber rattlesnakes could live in the Flat Tops but if they do, they're rare.

Livestock

Horses are not the only livestock you will encounter on the Flat Tops. You will also meet up with llamas, cattle, and sheep.

Usually, cows will run from you but not always. A cow with a calf is protective of her offspring. If she sees you as a threat, she will get belligerent, especially after being on the range all summer.

Bulls also present a problem. When cows are in heat, a bull has only one thing on his mind. A bull having amorous thoughts is an animal to avoid. If you're not a cow, he may see you as an object on which to express his aggression. Avoid them, even if you must go out of your way.

Sheep are also grazed in the wilderness, most often in the high meadows. Grazing is a historical use of the forests and was grandfathered into wilderness laws. You can reduce the probability of contacting livestock by inquiring at the appropriate district office to learn areas where sheep or cattle are being grazed.

There's one other hazard, but you are the only person who can prevent it. That's carelessness. Read the signs posted at trailheads. They inform you of wilderness regulations that protect both you and the resource. You don't need to go to the extremes that would be required by OSHA if they were to regulate wilderness travel but prudence is required. You go to the Flat Tops to enjoy the experience. Don't ruin it by doing something dumb. The wilderness is unforgiving of mistakes.

Altitude Illness

Anyone who visits the Flat Tops, whether you live in Colorado or the Gulf Coast, is a potential victim of altitude illness. A study several years ago found one in four visitors to a mountain resort had some altitude related symptoms.

Physical problems with altitude vary but can be grouped into three separate but related forms: Acute mountain sickness (AMS), high altitude pulmonary edema (HAPE), or fluid in the lungs, and high altitude cerebral edema (HACE), or fluid on the brain.

AMS is rarely seen below 6,500 feet. It becomes increasingly common above 8,000 feet, an elevation easily encountered on the Flat Tops. Symptoms are usually minor though they can be disabling.

Severity is greater among those who haven't taken time for acclimatization. A person making a rapid ascent may experience a headache—mild to severe—nausea, vomiting, shortness of breath, weakness, sleep disturbance, or experience periods of intermittent breathing.

Left untreated, AMS can advance to a serious, life-threatening illness, HAPE. It most often affects those who have had the problem previously, or have been acclimatized to high altitude, spent two or more weeks at low elevations, and then returned to high altitude. The symptoms can develop rather rapidly, in a matter of hours, or slowly over a period of one to three days. HAPE can occur with no symptoms of AMS.

A person suffering from HAPE will experience shortness of breath, irritating cough, weakness, rapid heart rate, and headache. The problem frequently gets worse at night. A pulse rate higher than 110 and respiration over sixteen breaths per minute is an early sign of HAPE. A medical emergency exists should the rates exceed a pulse of 120 and twenty breaths per minute. If the illness is untreated, the victim can go into a coma. Death may follow within a very short time.

A person with symptoms of HAPE must be immediately evacuated to lower altitude, preferably below 6,500 feet. Oxygen may help mild cases but descent is still necessary.

HACE is less common than the other forms of altitude illness but is the most serious. Symptoms include severe headache, confusion, hallucinations, unstable gait, loss of vision, loss of dexterity, and facial muscle paralysis. A sufferer may fall into a restless sleep, followed by deep coma and death. Immediate descent is required if the victim is to have any hope of recovery. Oxygen, if available, should be given by facemask at the rate of two to four liters per minute.

Symptoms of all three forms of altitude illness are progressive. Some are overlapping. It doesn't follow, however, that one form will always progress to another, more serious condition. A person can have HAPE or HACE without first showing symptoms of AMS.

Anyone showing signs of HAPE or HACE should be taken to lower altitude immediately. On the north side of the Flat Tops, the nearest medical facility is at Meeker. If you exit the wilderness by I-70, treatment is available at Glenwood Springs.

A person might think that a physical conditioning program would prevent altitude illness. It ain't so. Fitness will give you more endurance and aid in the efficient use of oxygen. But it won't prevent altitude problems. Even if your fitness level is excellent, don't let it lull you into overextending yourself before acclimatization.

A conditioning program should begin at least twelve weeks prior to traveling to high altitude. The body requires this length of time to respond to physical training. And remember that acclimatization is lost once a person has returned to low altitude (below 6,500 feet) after as little as ten days.

Even after completing a conditioning program, a person who lives near sea level is going to require time to acclimate to high altitude. When possible, you should allow two or three days to adjust to the altitude before engaging in any rigorous activity after arrival. Even then, you'll likely feel more tired than usual from normal activities. Smoking will decrease your performance at altitude and should be avoided.

Those who suffer from respiratory ailments such as asthma should be aware that the conditions could be aggravated by high altitude if not treated. Other ailments such as pulmonary hypertension may also be made worse. Anyone who uses medications for these conditions must also use them at altitude. One caution, though. The use of sedating antihistamines (the kind that make you drowsy) can decrease respiration while sleeping, worsening some symptoms of altitude illness.

Dehydration contributes to altitude sickness. Under ordinary conditions, the body needs about two to four quarts of water per day to stay hydrated. At altitudes above 8,000 feet, fluid requirements increase. Three or four quarts per day should be considered a minimum. Thirst is a poor indicator of need. Get lots of fluids and drink frequently. Avoid, or at least minimize, the use of beverages containing caffeine or alcohol as these contribute to dehydration.

Electrolyte replacement drinks are assimilated quickly. Those in powder form can be carried easily and mixed with water, ready for use as needed. Just make certain you get adequate fluids, whichever type you use. As long as your urine is colorless or very light yellow, you are sufficiently hydrated.

Some people are more susceptible to altitude illness than others. Medical help is available for this situation. Paul S. Auerbach, MD, MS, FACEP, FAWM, is the Redlich Family Professor of Surgery in the Division of Emergency Medicine at Stanford University School of Medicine. He is the world's leading medical expert on wilderness medicine and a prolific author. He is the editor of *Wilderness Medicine*, and author of *Medicine for the Outdoors* and *Field Guide to Wilderness Medicine*. The doctor's books are recommended for anyone who ventures into the backcountry.

Dr. Auerbach recommends the use of Diamox (acetazolamide) to aid acclimatization. A dose of 125 to 250 mg, taken twice daily, is advised beginning six to twelve hours before ascent and continued for twenty-four to forty-eight hours after reaching the maximum altitude. A prescription is required.

The drug does have some side effects. It will cause increased urination so get more fluids to stay hydrated. It can also cause tingling in your fingers and toes shortly after taking each dose. Taking the smaller dosage will reduce the frequency of urination. The tingling sensation shouldn't last very long. The symptoms, while annoying, are less so than altitude illness. One word of caution, though: Don't take this medication if you are allergic to sulfa drugs.

Minor headaches associated with AMS can be relieved with ordinary over-the-counter pain medications such as aspirin, acetaminophen, or ibuprofen. If you're having headaches, however, you may not be getting enough water. To prevent further difficulty, do not ascend to higher altitude until you are free of headache for twelve hours.

The best way a person can prepare for a high altitude adventure is to spend a lot of time at altitude. For the majority of us, this isn't practical. The next best thing is to prepare physically and mentally. Understanding acclimatization and getting yourself in top physical condition will improve your ability to meet the challenge of the Flat Tops and other high elevation travels.

3

MAPS FOR THE FLAT TOPS

Although the US Geological Survey publishes topographic maps (quads) that cover the Flat Tops Wilderness they are not the preferred quads to use. USGS quads covering the wilderness are more than thirty years old. The topography doesn't change significantly in that time but other features do. Roads, trails, and campgrounds that are built or abandoned may not appear on their quads.

The latest USFS map of the White River National Forest was completed in 1991 and is out of print. It shows surface ownership or control using color. This allows the wilderness traveler to know which land is public or private to avoid unintentional trespass.

The National Geographic Society (NGS) acquired Trails Illustrated (TI) of Evergreen, Colorado. They publish maps of the more popular recreational areas of the state. The USGS quads are used as a base. Data from many sources are incorporated to make a map showing the topography, drivable roads, current trails, and surface ownership. The maps are field checked and updated every few years, keeping them current. Each Trails Illustrated map incorporates eight to twelve USGS quads and is printed on durable plastic at a cost about one-fourth that of the survey quads covering the same area. The scale is 1:40,000, making a conveniently sized, weather-resistant map that fits in your pocket.

Each trail description in this guide lists the NGS TI map for that section.

Computer users who own map software can print maps to use on trails. NGS also publishes digital maps on CD-ROMs. These maps are available on a state basis for a reasonable price.

Maps included in this guide are intended to inform the reader of the wilderness area and its trails. The scale is not suitable for wilderness navigation.

Hiking the Flat Tops Wilderness Area

Because the Flat Tops Wilderness is large, it's a great place to get away from it all, by foot or horseback. Whether you plan a day hike or an extended backpack trip, you'll be able to find a trail that gives the experience you seek.

First of all, keep in mind that whichever trail you take, expect an ascent. With few exceptions, count on climbing at least a thousand feet to reach the plateau. One trail, 1825, ascends nearly 4,000 feet.

Once you're on top, though, the hike or horse ride is easy. The plateau is nearly flat and in some areas, you can hike several miles with no significant change in elevation. That doesn't mean it's absolutely level, though. Be aware of the contour interval. It's 40 feet, and as one hiker said, it can hide a lot of 39-foot anomalies.

If you've never used one, try taking a hiking staff. You'll be pleasantly surprised at the stability it gives when carrying a loaded backpack on rough, uneven terrain. Flat Tops trails are usually pretty good but in some places, cobbles and occasional boulders litter the trails. You will also appreciate a staff on steep trails. Using one can help you avoid a fall should you stumble on a rough section of the trail.

What should a hiker wear on the Flat Tops? That all depends on the season, but for summer, shorts and T-shirts work fine while walking. Nights on the plateau can get cool, though. If you live in the lowlands, it probably will seem cold. Carry long pants and a jacket for evenings in camp and a water-repellent parka and pants for rain. A baseball cap or boonie hat will protect your head from the sun and sunburn. Use sunscreen on exposed skin. The sun burns faster at high altitude.

Good sturdy boots are essential to enjoying your Flat Tops hike. You don't need heavy-duty climbing boots but you will need good support for carrying a heavy pack. Some of the new lightweight models should work fine here as long as they fit snuggly and provide good traction on wet clay soils. Gore-Tex® or similar liners will help keep your feet dry while crossing shallow streams and in the showers that occur frequently on the Flat Tops. Good water-resistant boots also allow you to practice low-impact hiking. Wilderness rangers recommend that you go ahead and slop through the mud on the trail. Walking on the trailside vegetation to keep dry contributes to erosion of the path.

Flat Tops Wilderness Trails

TRAIL DESCRIPTIONS

The trails are grouped by road access. Descriptions begin east of Meeker, in the northwest part of the Flat Tops.

For each trail, the *description* gives a brief synopsis of each trail. The *destination* tells what you'll find along the way and at the end of the trail. *Distances* given for trails are one way and are approximate. Time required for hiking a trail is not included as there are too many variables for an estimate to have meaning.

Elevations are given for the trailhead and trail end. In some cases, neither point is the high or low elevation for the trail so this is also included when it occurs somewhere else on the trail. GPS coordinates are given for each trail using both UTM and Latitude/Longitude (Lat/Lon). The bold type **13** for the UTM coordinates refers to the part of the UTM grid used in the Flat Tops.

Directions to the trailheads tell how to get there from the primary county or state road used as the heading for each section. Road designations vary depending on the source. All road numbers in this guide are from the 1991 White River National Forest map, the most recent edition. Road designations used on current Trails Illustrated maps, both paper and digital, show the latest road numbers or names. All trailheads are marked with signs. At wilderness boundaries, visitors are requested to sign the registers.

One point to keep in mind is that trails change over time. The Forest Service constructs new ones and abandons others. For this reason, always use the latest edition of any map.

The wilderness has a wide variety of trails, with distances varying from less than one-half mile to more than 25 miles. Difficulty varies with terrain but only a few have long, steep ascents. Trail 1825, the Oyster Lake Trail, begins about a mile south of Buford, and climbs more than 4,000 feet in the first 6 miles. From there to its junction with the Wall Lake Trail 1818, the hike is nearly level.

Another long trail also beginning south of Buford is the South Fork Trail 1827. From the South Fork Campground 10 miles south of Buford, it follows the South Fork of the White River to its headwaters. From the trailhead to the next point accessed by Forest Road 600, the trail climbs only a few hundred feet in 13 miles. For its entire length the trail follows a deep canyon, broad in some places, with a few short steep sections. For most of the way it's an easy hike. Until, that is, you pass the Doe Creek Trail. From there it isn't maintained so expect to find a few obstacles to get around.

Backpackers in search of other long hikes can do so by combining a few connecting trails. A person can begin near Sweetwater Lake on the south and go from there to Ripple Creek Pass on the north side by taking several connecting trails. Study wilderness maps to select a combination of trails to give a hike of a desired distance and destination.

For the person more interested in fishing rather than hiking more than a few miles, take the short hike from Forest Road 205 (the road to Trappers Lake) to Lake of the Woods. It's less than a half mile to some good brookie fishing. From Forest Road 900 west of Yampa a mile hike leads to Smith Lake. Stream fishermen will want to take Forest Road 600 to the Meadows to cast a fly in the South Fork. From the parking area it's only a couple hundred yards to the river. From there, fish up- or downstream. Anglers will find many other short hikes in this guide.

4

RIO BLANCO COUNTY ROAD 8

Trail descriptions begin at the town of Meeker, west of the wilderness, in Rio Blanco County. One mile north from town heading toward Craig on State Highway 13, go east on Rio Blanco County Road 8. This paved road follows the White River through ranch country and is the primary access to the north side of the wilderness. The Forest Service has designated the road between Meeker and Yampa as a Scenic Byway. Readers are advised to refer to maps in this guide or preferably the NGS Trails Illustrated maps while reading the trail descriptions.

From Meeker, head east 18 miles on County Road 8 to Buford just past County Road 17. Go south on County Road 17 a mile to County Road 10 to access the longest trail in the wilderness, the Oyster Lake Trail 1825. Turn east on County Road 10, which will lead south 9 miles to end at the South Fork Campground. Here backpackers and anglers can hike Trail 1827 along the South Fork of the White River. Between these two trails hikers can take four shorter trails that lead to the Flat Tops plateau.

Buford is an old community established more than a century ago. All that's left is the Buford Lodge, which is now permanently closed. East of Buford, Rio Blanco County Road 8 follows the North Fork of the White River upstream, to the east. It's 6 miles past Buford to County Road 12, which gives access to trails in the Marvine Creek area. Near the west end of County Road 8 and 12 are two trailheads, Papoose Creek Trail 2248 and Ute Creek Trail 1824. Both trails connect with Trail 1825 on the plateau. County Road 12 heads east along the south side of the North Fork 2 miles to an unnamed road that crosses the river to reconnect with County Road 8 by some now-closed businesses.

A mile east on County Road 12, Trail 1820 heads east along Big Ridge to Sable Lake. Or you can continue south on County Road 12 to trails that follow Marvine Creek: Trail 1823 to both Marvine Lakes, and Trail 1822 up the East Fork of Marvine Creek. Both connect to Trail 1825 after ascending to the plateau.

Continuing east 2 miles on County Road 8 from the junction of County Road 12 you come to the Lost Creek Guard Station and the end of the blacktop. Even though the road from here to the Routt County line is gravel, it's good, with a few washboard areas.

East 2 miles from Lost Creek Guard Station, the North Fork Campground is on the north, a good place to camp that's usually quiet. Another 6 miles takes you to Forest Road 205, the access to Trappers Lake.

County Road 8 continues east, climbing toward Ripple Creek Pass after passing Forest Road 205. A mile past the Trappers Lake Road the Picket Pin Trail 1811 makes a loop up to the plateau, and then down to the Trappers Lake Road.

Five miles past the Trappers Lake Road gets you to the Ripple Creek Overlook on the south. From this point, you have a broad view of the Flat Tops Wilderness. It's another mile to the 10,343-foot summit of the pass.

South Fork of the White River
Rio Blanco County Roads 17 and 10

Two and one-quarter miles east of the Lake Avery Dam, turn south off County Road 8 onto County Road 17. This rough road eventually joins Interstate 70 at New Castle about 39 miles south.

Turn left at the ranch buildings 1 mile south on County Road 17, which takes you to County Road 10. Turn east on County Road 10 and follow the South Fork of the White River, which meanders through the broad plain of glacially deposited sediments. Deer and elk will often be seen browsing in the hay meadows along the willow-lined stream. The South Fork Campground is at the end of County Road 10 about 11 miles from County Road 8.

OYSTER LAKE TRAIL 1825

UTM 13 027632E, 4427241N
Lat/Lon 39° 58′ 43.55″ N, 107° 37′ 6.10″ W

Description This is the longest trail on the Flat Tops. It connects with several others on the plateau, creating the possibility of many side trips. You could also exit the wilderness by any of these trails shown on USFS, NGS, and maps in this guide.

From the trailhead south of Buford, the route climbs quickly. Most of the 4,000-foot ascent occurs in the first 6 miles. Once you're on the plateau, the hike is much easier, at times nearly level. This is a good hike to experience the extensive size of the wilderness.

Destination Bailey Lake, Trails 1826, 2248, 2255, 2256, 1824, 1830, 1823 and 2259, 1822, 1819, 1818 on the Flat Tops plateau.

Distance 4.5 miles to Bailey Lake and Trail 1826, 6.5 to Trail 2248, 11.5 miles to Trail 2255, 12 miles to Trail 2256, 16 miles to Trail 1824, 19.5 miles to Trail 1830, 22.5 miles to Trails 1823 and 2259, 24 miles to Trail 1822, 26 miles to Trail 1819, 27 miles to Trail 1818.

Elevation 7,000 at trailhead, 11,300 a mile west of Lost Solar Park, 11,003 at Trail 1818

Directions to trailhead From Buford, drive 0.6 mile south on County Road 17. Park at the marked trailhead on west side of the road. Space is limited and your vehicle is exposed.

Maps Flat Tops NW, Flat Tops NE

The trail starts climbing as soon as you leave the county road and from there it's all uphill to Bailey Lake. In the 4 miles to the lake, the trail rises 1,800 feet. In the first couple of miles, you cross private land, so stay on the trail to avoid trespassing.

The first 2 or 3 miles take you through open ground and scattered stands of scrub brush. The trail crosses five intermittent creeks, that is, they're usually dry except during the spring thaw. You'll have about a mile of timber to walk through before breaking into a narrow opening for the last half mile to Trail 1826, which takes you beside Bailey Lake.

At the junction of 1826, Trail 1825 goes off to the east. A quarter-mile walk farther on Trail 1825 takes you to Swede Lake. Both lakes have open ground that's nearly level and suitable for camping. They're reported to have brook and rainbow trout to 12 inches.

The Oyster Lake Trail is one of the longest in the wilderness.

After leaving Swede Lake, Trail 1825 heads upward again, roughly following another intermittent drainage for a little more than a mile. Near the top of the draw, you can connect with Trail 2248, which will take you north down Papoose Creek.

From the junction with Trail 2248, 1825 trends southeast and takes you along the edge of the cliff face above Peltier Basin. You will want to take plenty of water on this stretch to prevent dehydration, as none is available along the trail.

As you ascend the gently sloping plateau, notice that the drop-off gradually increases from 600 feet, just above Swede Lake, to 1,200 feet where you view Peltier Lake, a mile to the west.

Hiking 5 miles south from Swede Lake on Trail 1825 takes you to the junction of Trail 2255, leading down Hill Creek. Clam Lake, the first available water along Trail 1825 after leaving Swede Lake, is a half mile farther south. From Clam Lake, the trail takes an easterly direction, where you walk in the open across a grassy flat. Near the next timber, Trail 2256 connects from the south.

Trail 1825 again enters the trees and descends a gentle slope. It emerges at Johnson Park, a long, narrow meadow a mile farther east on the trail. Here, you'll cross Ute Creek, which heads in Papoose Lake, a half mile to the south.

East of Johnson Park, the trail wanders through broken country, a mix of timber and open meadows. These areas can be good places to watch for elk. You will appreciate a pleasant feature of the Flat Tops on this part of the trail: it's nearly flat for 16 miles, having only moderate changes in elevation.

From Johnson Park east, the basalt-covered plateau is pock-marked with dozens of pothole lakes, their shallow depressions scraped out by Pleistocene glaciers. The next such lake you'll come to along the trail is Oyster Lake, a quarter mile north of Trail 1825 along

Trail 1824, which gives access to West Marvine and Ute Creeks to the north. If you want to camp here, try the timber on the northeast side.

Past the Trail 1824 junction, Trail 1825 still continues east through the same mix of timber and meadows. As you approach Lost Solar Park, the trail begins a moderate climb; nothing steep, though. You'll go past two small, unnamed peaks on the way to Trail 1830, which is about 4 miles from Oyster Lake. Near the first little molehill of a mountain, the trail reaches its zenith at 11,300 feet.

Lost Solar Park is a gently sloping, high alpine meadow. Glaciers have left the terrain rather lumpy. An abundance of moisture gives the grass a dark emerald color. July produces a plethora of wildflowers. There's a good chance of seeing elk here, either early or late in the day. At the east end of the park, a spur leads north to a group of unnamed lakes.

Past the park, Trail 1825 gets back into the timber, taking you beside several lakes tucked away in the trees and scattered about in nearby meadows. When the trail emerges from the timber, you'll come to Doe Creek Trail, 3 miles past the junction of Trail 1830. Going right here will take you down Doe Creek over Trail 2259. A few feet farther east, Trail 1823 will lead you 4 miles north down Marvine Creek past the Marvine Lakes. In this same area, you can connect with Trail 2259, leading down to the South Fork of the White River.

Continuing east, 1825 leads through alpine tundra, past more pothole lakes, and among stunted willows. Another 2 miles takes you to Trail 1822 and Twin Lakes. Each lake does have an island. Looking to the east from the lakes, you have a view of Trappers Peak, rising to a height of 12,002 feet. To the northwest is Big Marvine Peak, not quite as high but still impressive at 11,879 feet.

South of Twin Lakes, you'll see a low, broad, flat-topped hill, its slopes partially covered by timber. What you won't see from the trail are the several potholes on the top of the miniature plateau. This spot could make a good camp area as long as you keep your distance from the water.

Continuing east from Twin Lakes, the ground is nearly flat. A 1-mile stretch of trail crosses only a single contour line. This high plateau is also covered with pothole lakes, though of a lesser number than the area near Oyster Lake.

From Twin Lakes, it's only 2 more miles to Trail 1819. At this junction, look south and you see a low, timbered slope below Trappers Peak. Trail 1819 goes north past Big Fish Lake and to Himes Peak Campground. Hidden south of Trail 1825 is Star Lake, the largest of several shallow glacially scoured potholes. There's no trail there but you'll find Star Lake easily by heading south toward Trappers Peak, staying in the open alpine meadow until you reach the outlet stream flowing east from Star Lake.

A mile past Trail 1819 to Big Fish Lake, you come to Trail 1818. From this junction, it's 3 miles to Trappers Lake, all downhill, or 2 miles south to Wall Lake.

Campsites along Trail 1825—the longest trail on the Flat Tops— are available at any flat ground where you want to set up your tent. Just be sure to stay at least 100 feet from the trail or water.

PELTIER LAKE TRAIL 1826

UTM 13 0283323 E, 4419223 N
Lat/Lon 39° 53' 50.63" N, 107° 32' 4.02" W

Description The trail traverses a timbered slope below the plateau. It's not actually inside the wilderness but it is close to the boundary. There's a short, steep climb at the beginning of the hike. This trail lets you observe the variety of vegetation across the Flat Tops. Much of this hike leads through scrub oak and low willows growing on the lower, west-facing slopes.

Destination Peltier Lake, Trail 1825

Distance 3 miles to Peltier Lake, 6 miles to Trail 1825

Elevation 7,590 at trailhead; 8,892 at Trail 1825

Directions to trailhead On County Road 10, 8 miles south from County Road 17 to the marked trailhead on the east side of the road. Parking is available 200 yards south on the east side of the road.

In just a few feet from the trailhead, the path disappears into the trees and begins climbing as it traverses a narrow ridge and a moderately steep, but short, slope. To the east, you'll see a nearly vertical wall rising more than 1,000 feet to the plateau of the Flat Tops. Below you to the west, you have a view of the South Fork valley and the meandering stream as it flows south to join the North Fork. After 3 miles of climbing through scrub oak and low trees, you come to Peltier Lake at the west end of Peltier Basin.

Maps Flat Tops NW

The lake is shallow but is reported to have brook and rainbow trout. The north and west side of the shoreline is flat, good for camping. The tree line on the northeast, being farther from the trail, may be the best site. East of the lake and 200 feet higher, you'll find a few small ponds hidden in a clearing. One-half mile north of the lake is a meadow where you should be able to camp away from the ponds.

From Peltier Lake, the trail continues north, traversing the west-facing slope and crossing several intermittent drainages. The last mile of the trail to Bailey Lake is across a flat, marshy in places, as it cuts through the timber. The path connects with Trail 1825 a hundred yards north of the lake.

HILL CREEK TRAIL 2255

UTM 13 0283727E, 4418877N
Lat/Lon 39° 53' 39.30"N, 107° 31' 46.39" W

Description This route takes you on a constant climb as you work your way up the scrub-covered lower slopes and timbered high country. It generally follows Hill Creek to the plateau.

Destination Trail 1825

Distance 4 miles

Elevation 8,010 at trailhead; 10,657 at Trail 1825

Directions to trailhead From the junction of County Road 17 and County Road 10, drive 8.8 miles south on County Road 10. Forest Service sign on the left reads "Hill Creek Trail Head 1 Mile. High Clearance Vehicles Only." The road is fine as long as it's dry. Trail 2255 heads east, uphill, from the parking area.

Maps Flat Tops NW

The trailhead is a large parking area in the open surrounded by aspen groves, and lodgepole and spruce forest. There's plenty of room here to park a pickup and horse trailer if you prefer riding to walking the trails. The trail begins at the east end of the parking area. One-half mile east of the trailhead, you cross Hill Creek Trail, then head up a steep slope north of the stream. Be aware that this trail is not found on the USGS quad.

After crossing the small stream, the path stays above the creek as you climb the steep slope. After 3 miles, the grade moderates before beginning the final climb to the plateau. From the top, it follows one of the drainages that is the head of Hill Creek. The walk through the long, narrow meadow is easy, ascending only about 200 feet between the rim and Trail 1825. The wilderness boundary is at the rim. From there, it's a mile north to the trail junction, which is a short distance northwest of Clam Lake.

This trail climbs fast but is a shorter route to the top and Trail 1825.

FOWLER CREEK TRAIL 2256

UTM 13 0283674 E, 4418809 N
Lat/Lon 39° 53' 37.40" N, 107° 31' 49.01" W

Description This steep trail follows Fowler Creek. It takes you into the wilderness and eventually connects with Trail 1825 near Clam Lake.

Destination Head of Fowler Creek

Distance 6 miles

Elevation 8,010 at trailhead; 11,102 at Eastview; 10,690 at Trail 1825

Directions to trailhead From the junction of County Road 17 and County Road 10, drive 8.8 miles south on County Road 10. Forest Service sign on the left reads "Hill Creek Trail Head 1 Mile. High Clearance Vehicles Only." The road is fine as long as it's dry. At the parking area, the road makes a loop to the west. Trail 2256 begins at the west end of the loop, where it heads uphill south, then turns east near the summit of the low ridge.

Maps Flat Tops SW

Fowler Creek joins Hill Creek about one-half mile east of the trailhead. It's a small, fast stream flowing down a narrow draw. The Fowler Creek Trail shares the trailhead with the Hill Creek Trail. The path wanders through the timber a short distance as it climbs the nose of a broad ridge above Fowler Creek. It soon crosses an open slope as it heads uphill southeast toward Wilbur Lake, 2 miles from the trailhead.

A mile farther east, the path becomes steeper as it reaches the headwall of the small draw drained by Fowler Creek. As it ascends to the plateau, you climb 600 feet in little more than a half mile.

Near the rim of the wilderness plateau, the trail enters a meadow and the climb moderates as it leads through meadows broken by scattered stands of timber. A mile from the rim, the ascent flattens, following a low draw to the high point on the trail, a summit named Edgeview. It overlooks a 200-foot drop-off to the east.

From here, you continue north, where the trail enters another long, narrow meadow after a half-mile walk. The trail joins Trail 1825 after another mile, at the west end of Bailey Lake.

FOWLER RIM TRAIL 2257

UTM 13 0283674 E, 4418809 N
Lat/Lon 39° 53′ 37.40″ N, 107° 31′ 49.01″ W

Description The Fowler Rim Trail travels over a scrub oak hillside before beginning a strenuous climb as it traverses the west side of Fowler Peak. The trail follows the rim above the South Fork of the White River offering spectacular views to the south. Dominant tree species along the trail include Engelmann spruce and alpine fir. The trail also crosses through open parks with small aspen stands. The Fowler Rim Trail ends where it meets the Fowler Creek Trail 2256—a little more than 5 miles from the trailhead.

Destination Fowler Creek Trail 2256

Distance 5.2 miles

Elevation 8,010 at trailhead; 10,343 at Fowler Creek Trail 2256

Directions to trailhead From the junction of County Road 17 and County Road 10, drive 8.8 miles south on County Road 10. Forest Service sign on the left reads "Hill Creek Trail Head 1 Mile. High Clearance Vehicles Only." The road is fine as long as it's dry. At the parking area, the road makes a loop to the west. Trail 2256 begins at the west end of the loop, where it heads uphill south, then turns east near the summit of the low ridge.

Maps Flat Tops SW, Flat Tops SE

Fowler Creek joins Hill Creek about one-half mile east of the trailhead. It's a small fast stream flowing down the narrow draw. The Fowler Creek Trail shares the trailhead with the Hill Creek Trail. The path wanders through the timber a short distance as it climbs the nose of a broad ridge above Fowler Creek. It soon crosses an open slope as it heads uphill southeast toward Wilbur Lake, 2 miles from the trailhead. A mile farther east, the path becomes steeper as it reaches the headwall of the small draw drained by Fowler Creek. As it ascends to the plateau, you climb 600 feet in little more than a half mile.

Near the rim of the wilderness plateau, the trail enters a meadow and the climb moderates as it leads through meadows broken by scattered stands of timber. A mile from the rim, the ascent flattens, following a low draw to a high point on the trail named Edgeview. It overlooks a 200-foot drop-off to the east.

From here, you continue north, where the trail enters another long meadow after a half-mile walk. The trail joins Trail 1825.

SOUTH FORK TRAIL 1827

UTM 13 0293317 E, 4415598 N
Lat/Lon 39° 51′ 53.15 N, 107° 31′ 59.57″ W

Description An easy hike. The trail climbs only 1,400 feet in 13 miles as it follows the South Fork of the White River, emerging from the deep canyon at a place named the Meadows. It can be hiked in either direction at the Meadows.

Destination Trail 1828, Trail 1829, the Meadows, Trail 1838, Trail 1830, Trail 2259, Trail 1816

Distance 5 miles to Trail 1828, 7 miles to Trail 1829, 13.7 miles to the Meadows, 23.25 miles to Trail 1838, 25 miles to Trail 1830, 25.5 miles to Trail 1816

Elevation 7,602 at the trailhead; 9,000 at the Meadows; 10,903 at Trail 1816

Directions to trailhead From the junction of County Road 17 and County Road 10, drive 10 miles south on County Road 10 to South Fork Campground (the end of the road). Park in the designated area south of the campground near the trailhead. A sign marks the trailhead, where hikers can register.

Maps Flat Tops SW, Flat Tops NE

The trail begins at the entrance to a deep, narrow canyon carved in massive limestone. It follows the course of the South Fork of the White

The trail follows the South Fork of the White River for about 14 miles to the Meadows. Good fishing all the way.

River, leading you upstream and exiting the gorge at the Meadows, 13 miles up the river.

After leaving the trailhead, you walk beside one of the most beautiful streams in the state. Following the runoff, the water is clear, flowing over a bed of black and red basalt, and white limestone boulders. The stream is broad, having numerous deep holes, hiding places for trout. If you approach the water carefully, you'll also see rainbow and cutthroat that occasionally rise to inhale a tasty-looking insect from the surface. A few feet from the parking area is a wooden bridge crossing the river giving access to the South Fork's west bank.

About 3 miles from the campground, the river narrows, being squeezed by the canyon walls, as it plunges over a short series of cascades. Be sure to take your camera for this scenic spot.

Above the cascades, the canyon opens a bit and the stream channel broadens. Another 2 miles of easy walking takes you to Lost Solar Creek and Trail 1828. The land and cabins here are private, the ownership dating back years prior to the creation of the wilderness. The area is marked. Through this section, you must stay on the trail to avoid trespassing.

A mile upstream from Lost Solar Park, the trail wanders through timber at the bottom of the deep gorge. Another mile takes you to Park Creek and Trail 1829, which follows the creek up to the plateau.

Above Park Creek, the canyon walls become steeper, nearly vertical in appearance. Here, the trail wanders a short distance from the river, far enough that you'll miss an especially scenic narrow section of the canyon, about 8 miles from the trailhead. Here, the stream has cut a trough through the resistant granite. It's an angler's frustration. The long narrow pool that is formed, a few feet off the trail, is deep, too deep to easily wade. Steep granite walls make the water difficult to reach from either side. The pool is photogenic, though.

In this narrow portion of the canyon, the river meanders, runs through shallow riffles, and plunges over boulders. Deep pools form at bends, creating trout holding water. A little farther upstream, the gradient increases and willows growing along either bank make it difficult to approach the water, which is very frustrating if you're an angler. A little farther upstream is a small falls, not very high but large enough to be noted on topo maps. Above the falls, the gradient flattens and the trail climbs less steeply. Near the falls is a wooden gate across the trail in what seems an unlikely place. Just be sure to close it after passing.

The final 3 miles of the trail is an easy walk past lush meadows and vertical limestone walls. The climb is only 120 feet in that distance. Aspen groves shade the bench above the river. You pass through several more gates along the way. Across from the Budges Flattops Wilderness Lodge, near the end of your hike, is a fenced enclosure in which the resort sometimes keeps horses. Be sure to close the gates so the horses don't wander.

Backpackers will find plenty of places to camp. Be sure to stay at least 100 feet from the water.

Also across from the resort, the trail weaves through a patch of willows that grow along an unnamed trickle coming off the plateau from the north. The tiny stream has sufficient flow to flood the trail here but by clinging to the edge of the path and the brush, you can keep your feet dry.

From here, it's less than a half mile to the Meadows. A wooden footbridge takes you across the river to a parking lot west of the Meadows.

Camping along the river is a pleasant experience and there are many sites along the trail. The sound of the water is relaxing and soothing. Pick your site with care, though. High ground is suggested as heavy rains upstream can raise the water level quickly. Also, remember the 100-foot distance from water to your camp. The only exception to open camping is the area at Lost Solar Creek, which is private land.

After passing Nichols Creek and Doe Creek, the trail turns east continuing to follow the South Fork out of the canyon onto the Flat Tops plateau, ending at the Trappers Lake Trail 1816 near Shingle Peak. The section of trail above Doe Creek is not maintained and hikers can expect additional challenges due to deadfall and swampy areas.

Access to the river along the first mile, near the Meadows, is a challenge. From the trail, the willows growing along the White don't look bad. They're almost impenetrable, though. Deer like to hide in the thickets. The dense cover provides concealment and browse for them close to water.

Above the river, the canyon walls rise, gently at first, then nearly vertically. The lower slopes are open, covered with high grasses and low brush here and there. The ground is hummocky in places along the river, the result of unstable conditions created when the glaciers left behind piles of rubble in the valley. You'll also find ponds scattered along the river. Approach them quietly and you may catch a glance at a mama teal and her babies, hatched in the early summer.

Water is abundant along this trail. There are springs along the west bank a couple of miles upstream from the Doe Creek trail junction. On the east bank, several tiny streams come rushing down the steep sides to join the White.

SOUTH FORK TRAIL 1827 HEADING WEST

From Eagle County Road 301 2 miles north of I-70, Forest Road 600 takes you to the Meadows, and Budge's Flattops Wilderness Lodge a mile to the west. Forest Road 600 is a rough dusty road. From County Road 301 it's 38 miles to the Meadows and 39 miles to Budge's Flattops Wilderness lodge. Anglers will want to take lightweight waders to fish the river. Several pleasant campsites are found along the trail.

Destination Trail 1829, Trail 1828, South Fork Trailhead

Distance 6.7 miles to Trail 1829, 11.7 miles to Trail 1828, 13.7 miles to the trailhead at the South Fork Campground

Elevation 9,000 at the Meadows; 7,602 at the South Fork Campground trailhead

Directions to trailhead From Eagle County Road 301 2 miles north of I-70, Forest Road 600 takes you west to the Meadows.

LOST SOLAR TRAIL 1828

UTM 13 028988 E, 4415187 N
Lat/Lon 39° 51' 45.27" N, 107° 27' 23.23 W

Description This trail follows a canyon that shows the contrasting geology of the Flat Tops. The canyon was formed by faulting and erosion rather than by glaciers. It's a long, but not too steep, climb except in a few places.

Destination Trail 1830, Lost Solar Park

Distance 7 miles

Elevation 7,904 at Trail 1827, 10,750 at Trail 1830

Directions to trail From the junction of County Road 17 and County Road 10, drive 10 miles south on County Road 10 to South Fork Campground (park at the end of the road where a sign indicates the wilderness boundary). From the South Fork Campground, take Trail 1827 along the South Fork of the White River upstream 5 miles to the junction with Lost Solar Trail 1828.

You can also reach 1828 from the Meadows (see description of South Fork Trail 1827), and from Trail 1830 (see description of Nichols Creek Trail 1830) on the plateau.

Maps Flat Tops NE

Steep-sided walls are a prominent feature found in the South Fork of the White River canyon. From the bottom, access to the plateau appears off-limits to hikers. Fortunately, incisions have been made in the rugged landscape, the result of fracturing and erosion of the rock. During the construction of the Flat Tops faulting broke the rock. Natural processes of weathering enlarged these fractures, creating V-shaped canyons, in contrast to the U-shaped valley of the South Fork, formed by moving layers of ice. Lost Solar Creek is one of the drainages formed by faulting of the rock. The resultant valley offers the hiker relatively easy access to the top.

The trail begins at the confluence of Lost Solar Creek and the South Fork, among a group of cabins. The land here is private so stay on the trail. It follows the creek along the bottom of the deep V-shaped canyon. Because of the steep sides, there are few suitable campsites until you are 5 miles up the trail from the South Fork. Here at the confluence of Lost Solar and a small, unnamed creek that heads in the small canyon to the north, the ground is flat enough for camping.

The grade is gentle most of the way up as the path traverses the north side of the canyon. Past the confluence of Lost Solar Creek and the unnamed stream, the trail climbs again, a bit more steeply this time. It finally emerges from the canyon in sight of Timber Mountain and Lost Solar Park. Here you connect with Trail 1830.

Campsites are limited along this trail but once you are on the flat, you will find meadows where you'll want to set up your tent. Look for places to camp around Timber Mountain.

PARK CREEK TRAIL 1829

UTM 13 0292116 E, 4414356 N
Lat/Lon 39° 51' 20.46" N, 107° 25' 48.12" W

Description Similar to Lost Solar Trail 1828 but a bit shorter.

Destination Park Creek, Trail 1830

Distance 5 miles to the head of Park Creek and Trail 1830

Elevation 8,131 at the South Fork; 10,430 at Trail 1830

Directions to trail From the junction of County Road 17 and County Road 10, drive 10 miles south on County Road 10 to South Fork Campground (park at the end of the road where a sign indicates the wilderness boundary). From the South Fork Campground, take Trail 1827 along the South Fork of the White River upstream about 7 miles to the junction with Park Creek Trail 1829. You can also reach 1829 from Budge's Flattops Wilderness Lodge on Trail 1827 (see description of South Fork Trail 1827).

Maps Flat Tops NE

Park Creek descends another canyon created by faulting of the plateau. The trail departs the South Fork in a broad area of the valley and climbs rather abruptly for the first half mile before leveling out. For the next 3 miles, the ascent is gradual as the path meanders through the trees and open meadows while crossing the creek several times. As you approach the head of the canyon, the trail gets steeper. Near the upper end of the canyon you'll find a falls. It's not large, but it is scenic. The last mile ascends quickly, requiring switchbacks to get up the steep headwall before you emerge on the flat. A short walk through the open meadow takes you to Trail 1830. If you want to camp along the trail, you'll find places in the wooded flat middle section of the canyon.

FAWN CREEK TRAIL 1838

UTM 13 301647 E, 4413491 N
Lat/Lon 39° 51′ 01″ N, 107° 19′ 06″ W

Description This is an alternate route to Shepherd and Rim Lakes. For the backpacker, it won't save time or miles. Used mainly for horse travel.

Destination Elk Knob, Trail 1816

Distance 4 miles to Elk Knob, 6 miles to Trail 1816

Elevation 9,095 at the parking area; 10,600 at Trail 1816

Directions to trailhead From Eagle County Road 301 (Colorado River Road), drive west on Eagle County Road 17 at Deep Creek, which

Forest Road 600 stops here at the Meadows and gives access to the upper South Fork of the White River and more good fishing. You will also find places to camp.

becomes Forest Road 600 at the National Forest boundary. Thirty-eight miles from County Road 301 to the Meadows and the trailhead. A sign marks the wilderness boundary. Park just off the forest road.

Maps Flat Tops NE

The trail begins at the sign marking the wilderness boundary by the road. There is no information there concerning the trail. Look directly east and you'll notice the barely discernible path. A few feet farther, the path crosses Fawn Creek (a tiny trickle), the stream directly north of the parking area. The best way to find the trail is to cross the creek, then follow the trail up the slope. There, the trail is more distinct.

The trail climbs the steep slope as it follows Fawn Creek to the creek's source on the plateau. You walk in the open most of the way until you reach the top of the slope. From there, you can head east, going cross-country to connect with Trail 1816, and head north to Shepherd and Rim Lakes. Budge's Flattops Wilderness Lodge uses this route for horseback trips to the lakes, so you can follow the horse path to the trail.

NICHOLS CREEK TRAIL 1830

UTM 13 301178 E, 4416047 N
Lat/Lon 39° 52' 22.93" N, 107° 19' 29.43" W

Description This trail is 2 miles of climbing followed by 3 miles of pleasant, nearly level hiking. The trail gets a lot of horse traffic from Budge's Flattops Wilderness Lodge.

Destination Trail 1829, Trail 1828, Trail 1825

Distance 2 miles to Trail 1829, 4 miles to Trail 1828, 5 miles to Trail 1825

Elevation 9,170 at the South Fork; 11,018 at Trail 1825

Directions to trail Hike 2 miles north from the Meadows along Trail 1827. At the junction of Trail 1827 and Trail 1830, this trail begins at Nichols Creek and heads west up the steep slope. The sign at the trailhead may show the name as "Nichole" Creek.

Maps Flat Tops NE

You'll have to make a stream crossing to reach this trail. The difficult part is keeping your feet dry. The White River isn't large here but it's still too wide to jump. Unless you have waders along, it's probably best

The Flat Tops has the largest elk herd in the state, making it a popular destination for hunters in the fall.

to remove your boots and wade across. The trail sign is on the west side of the river.

Nichols Creek is a small trickle of water that plunges in a nearly straight line down the canyon wall. The trail is a steep climb that follows close by on the north side of Nichols Creek. There are few meanders on the steep route but the hike isn't as bad as it seems. The hillside is open, covered in grass and low brush. There are a couple of bogs to cross. One has timbers placed in the muck so you won't sink in too deep. You pass beside light timber on the way up in a few places. Near the head of the small drainage, the slope begins to ease. It gives the feeling of seeing the light at the end of the tunnel. You're almost there.

At the rim, the walk is suddenly easy, having a nearly imperceptible gradient. A small pond awaits on top, an inviting place to sit and recover from your exertion. Here, you connect with Trail 1829, which leads west along Park Creek. The plateau area south of Trail 1830 has a large number of pothole lakes. If you're interested in fishing, check with the Colorado Parks and Wildlife for expected conditions and to learn if any have been stocked.

Continuing past the pond, Trail 1830 wanders westward through large, grassy parks. It climbs slightly but the hike now is easy. As the route veers north, you come in view of Timber Mountain on the right, east of the trail. It rises to 11,425 feet but doesn't appear impressive since it's only 600 feet to the top. Directly west of the peak and left of the trail lies Horseshoe Lake. Get to it from the small clearing. You'll have a quarter-mile hike from the trail through the timber to the lake.

Past Timber Mountain, the trail continues north, leading to the junction with Trail 1828, Lost Solar Creek, and Lost Solar Park. One mile past Trail 1828, you reach Trail 1825.

Finding a campsite along this trail won't be a problem.

Once you're on the plateau, you'll be in elk country. The dense timber gives good cover, where they go to rest and chew their cuds after feeding in the many grassy parks.

DOE CREEK TRAIL 2259

UTM 13 301488 E, 4416969 N
Lat/Lon 39° 52′ 53.33″ N, 107° 19′ 17.08″ W

Description This hike takes you to the open country in the heart of the Flat Tops Plateau. On top, this route connects with Trail 1823, which leads down Marvine Creek.

Destination Trail 1825, Trail 1823

Distance 5 miles

Elevation 9,200 at the South Fork of the White River; 10,954 at junction with Trail 1825

Directions to trail From Eagle County Road 301 2 miles north of I-70, Forest Road 600 takes you to the Meadows, and Budge's Flattops Wilderness Lodge a mile to the west. Forest Road 600 is a rough dusty road. From County Road 301 it's 38 miles to the Meadows and 39 miles to Budge's Flattops Wilderness lodge. Anglers will want to take lightweight waders to fish the river. Several pleasant campsites are found along the trail.

Hike 2 miles north from the Meadows along Trail 1827. At the junction and past the Nichols Creek Trail, Trail 2259 begins beside Doe Creek and ascends a grassy slope to the north.

Maps Deep Lake

**Stick a camera in your backpack. The wilderness has
many photogenic spots.**

As on the Nichols Creek Trail, you must cross the river to reach this one, too. On the west bank, the trail continues upstream along the South Fork to Doe Creek. Here, the trail leaves the river and begins a gentle climb up and across a grassy slope.

About a mile from the river, you pass a small patch of timber, and then continue on across the hillside. Along the way, you pass a few springs below the trail. The next mile is a bit steeper as the path zig-zags up the slope toward the head of a small, unnamed drainage. A half mile farther, you break out on top of the plateau.

The next 3 miles are easy—a casual stroll leading past a surface pockmarked with potholes. In that distance, the trail rises about 200 feet, then falls about 50 or so feet as you descend to cross the headwaters of Doe Creek.

At the confluence of Doe Creek and the South Fork, an old, no longer maintained trail follows Doe Creek upstream. Doe Creek Falls, a scenic place worth the detour, is located 2 miles from the South Fork north along this path. The waterfall isn't high, only about 20 or 30 feet. The scene is worth the walk though. The water plunges over a cleft in the black basalt. The grassy hillside downstream from the falls is a good place to see elk.

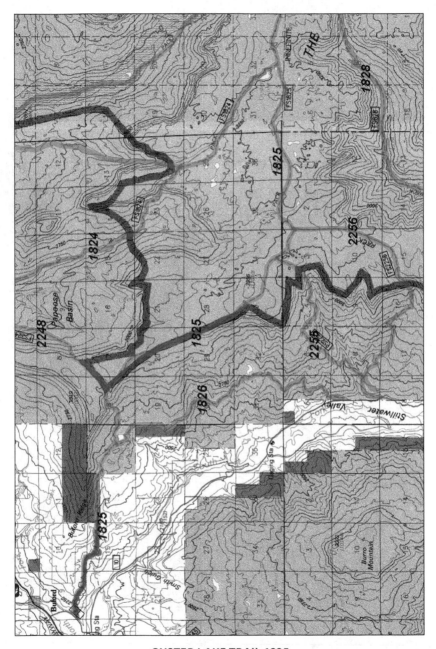

OYSTER LAKE TRAIL 1825

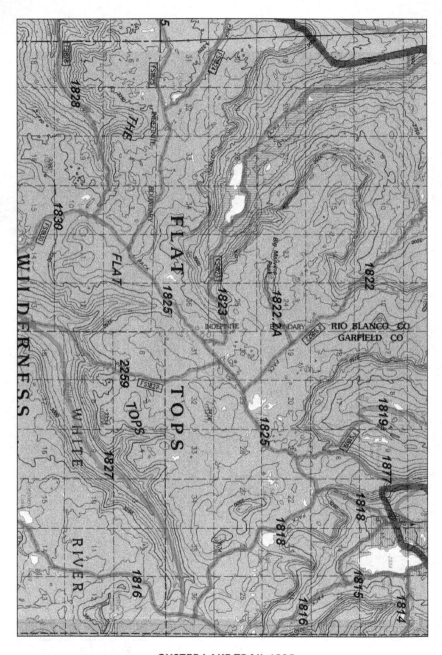

OYSTER LAKE TRAIL 1825

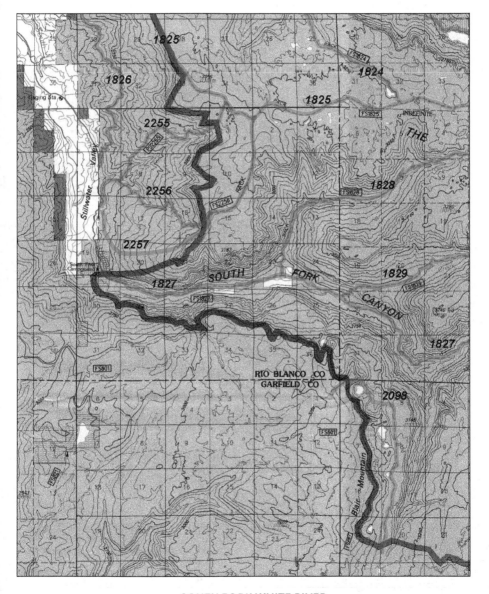

SOUTH FORK WHITE RIVER

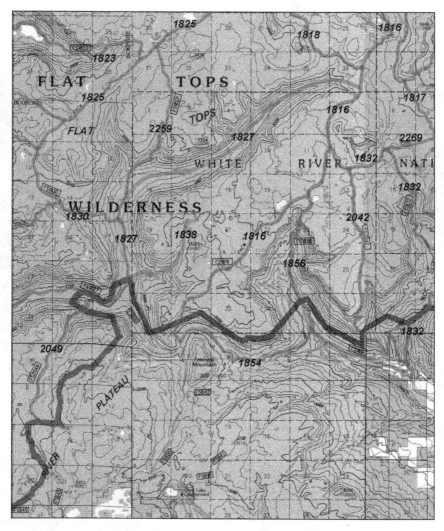

UPPER SOUTH FORK WHITE RIVER

5

NORTH FORK OF THE WHITE RIVER (COUNTY ROADS 8 AND 12)

PAPOOSE CREEK TRAIL 2248

UTM 13 0286405 E, 4433442 N
Lat/Lon 40° 1′, 33.83″ N, 107° 30′ 11.26″ W

Description The trail follows Papoose Creek the first 2 miles, leading through dense timber and narrow meadows along the creek. The hike takes you through Papoose Basin before ascending the steep wall to the west, giving access to the wilderness boundary on the plateau.

Destination Trail 1825

Distance 9 miles

Elevation 7,630 at trailhead; 9,920 at Trail 1825

Directions to trailhead From Buford drive 6 miles east on County Road 8, then go right on County Road 12. Continue 1 mile east to County Road 119. Turn right, south, about 1 mile to a junction. Continue straight ahead, south, to the trailhead parking area on the left, 0.7 mile from County Road 12. The trailhead is located 0.25 mile past the parking area, left of the entrance to Ute Lodge. The 1991 White River National Forest map shows conflicting road designations to this trailhead.

The Papoose Creek Trail leads past Nimerick Point, the western most promontory of the Flat Tops Plateau.

Maps Flat Tops NW, Flat Tops NE

This trail begins by following Papoose Creek up its small, timbered draw for the first mile. After climbing to 8,800 feet, Trail 2248 enters Papoose Basin, a small park with scattered stands of timber and sloping meadows. Looking to the west, you'll see a steep wall, rising some 700 feet. The trail leads up that wall. The trail turns gradually to the west and climbs a series of switchbacks out of Papoose Basin onto Nimerick Point, the western most promontory of the Flat Tops plateau.

Once on top, though, the walk is just a stroll through the meadow across a narrow plateau, where you connect with Trail 1825 and enter the wilderness. Once you connect with this trail, you can head east to reach Marvine Lakes, Wall Lake, or Trappers Lake. Or head west to County Road 17.

Carry plenty of water. There's none available past Papoose Creek.

UTE CREEK TRAIL 1824

UTM 13 0287000 E, 4432888 N
Lat/Lon 40° 1′ 16.32″ N, 107° 29′ 44.74 W

Description This route parallels Ute Creek to the wilderness boundary 5 miles from the trailhead. Much of the trail is up a moderate grade until reaching the steep wall leading to the plateau. Here, the ascent is steep but short. The trail soon crosses West Marvine Creek and follows it to Oyster Lake and Trail 1825.

Destination West Marvine Trail (Abandoned), Trail 1825

Distance West Marvine Trail 7 miles, Trail 1825 9 miles

Elevation 7,693 at trailhead; 10,705 at junction with Trail 1825

Directions to trailhead From Buford drive 6 miles east on County Road 8, then, go right on County Road 12. Continue 1 mile east to County Road 119. Turn right and drive south a half mile. Go left on an undesignated Forest Road to a group of privately owned summer cabins. Park on the west beside Ute Creek, then walk south on the road to the trailhead beside the bridge.

Maps Flat Tops NE

The Ute Creek Trailhead is just outside the Ute Creek summer home group. This trail takes you on one of the higher climbs of any in the Flat Tops, nearly 3,000 feet. Immediately after leaving the parking area, you'll enter the first of many long but narrow meadows as you begin your ascent.

The Ute Creek Fire burned trees along several miles of the trail in 1994. The trail connects with Trail 1825 on top.

The first half of the trail closely follows Ute Creek. The stream is small, its banks lined with brush. It does have challenging fishing for brookies and cutthroats, though. You climb for about one-half mile on switchbacks to the top of the ridge between Ute Creek and Campbell Creek.

You enter the wilderness 7 miles from the trailhead. So far, the climb has been steady but not steep. For the next 2 miles, the climb gets more serious, rising 1,200 feet, 600 of which occurs in the last half mile. Once you're on top, though, the walk is easy. The Ute Creek Fire of 1994 burned the trees along several miles of trail. Be extremely careful around standing dead trees.

Near the junction with the West Marvine Trail west of the trail are more than a dozen pothole lakes. The ground is mostly flat, making for good campsites near the trees.

You'll come to the abandoned West Marvine Trail, which leads down West Marvine Creek to Marvine Campground, 7 miles from the trailhead. Continuing on south, the trail stays in the open the last 2.5 miles, leading past Oyster Lake and to Trail 1825.

WEST MARVINE CREEK TRAIL 1868 (ABANDONED)

UTM 13 0292936 E, 4431569 N
Lat/Lon 40° 0' 39.24" N, 107° 25' 33.98" W

Description This trail has two trailheads. The south trailhead originates at the Marvine Creek Campground and connects with West Marvine Creek after a mile of climbing the moderate slope along House Creek. The north trailhead takes off from the Ute Creek Trailhead but heads east across some private property before turning southeast. It links up with the south half of the trail at House Creek. From this junction the trail continues south along West Marvine Creek nearly 5 miles to the junction with Ute Creek Trail 1824.

Destination West Marvine Creek, Trail 1824

Distance 7 miles to Trail 1824

Elevation 8,081 at trailhead; 8,900 at end of maintained portion

Directions to South trailhead At Buford drive 8 miles east on County Road 8. Go southeast across the bridge on County Road 12. Drive 2 miles to the point where the road turns south and follows Marvine Creek. Drive 4 more miles to the trailhead. From the Marvine Trail parking lot take the right fork west across the road past the camp-ground to the trail.

Directions to North trailhead Near Ute Lodge by the Ute Creek Trailhead.

Maps Flat Tops NE

MARVINE TRAIL 1823

UTM 13 0292936 E, 4431569 N
Lat/Lon 40° 0′ 39.24″ N, 107° 25′ 33.98″ W

Description This is another trail that gets you onto the plateau. It's not a difficult hike, as the trail has only a few moderately steep sections as it ascends the scenic, glacially carved valley. Be sure to take your fishing rod as there are numerous places to fish along the way. This is a popular trail for horse pack trips. On top, you can take your choice of several trails for a different return route.

Destination Slide Lake, lower Marvine Lake, upper Marvine Lake, Trail 1825

Distance 5 miles to Slide Lake, 6 miles to lower Marvine Lake, 7 miles to upper Marvine Lake, 11 miles to Trail 1825

Elevation 8,160 at trailhead; 10,954 at junction with Trail 1825

Directions to trailhead From Buford drive 6 miles east on County Road 8, then go right on County Road 12. Cross the bridge on County Road 12 and head east for 3 miles where the road turns south and follows Marvine Creek. Park at the trailhead. There is also a place to unload horse trailers. The trailhead is 5.5 miles past the bridge over Marvine Creek. The trail begins south of the horse corral. Here you will see a sign and a place to register.

Maps Flat Tops NE

Begin at the trailhead near the horse loading area on the east side of the road in sight of the campground. It's optional but wilderness travelers are requested to sign the register at the trailhead sign. Follow the path south across a couple of small ridges, which fortunately are not too high or steep, giving you a chance to adjust to the load on your back. After about a mile, the trail descends slightly to follow Marvine Creek.

The gradual climb along Marvine Creek is not difficult. Much of the way, you walk in the open below a timbered slope (above you to

Hiking builds an appetite, so pack a lunch.

the east) and below nearly vertical walls. Marvine Creek is in view to the west most of the way. It's a small stream that is home to small brook, cutthroat, and rainbow trout. A few ponds create deep holes for the fish. The water is clear, though, and a careful approach is needed to avoid spooking them when the surface is smooth.

Five miles from the trailhead, you come to Slide Lake, looking much like a giant beaver pond, which it isn't. The lake is full of brookies to 8 or 9 inches, all eager to hit a fly. The clarity of the water is deceitful. You won't be able to wade out very far, even with hip boots.

To the east above Slide Lake, you'll be able to see the steep buttresses forming the foundation for Rat Mountain, its summit reaching above 11,000 feet. Early in the summer, you'll see waterfalls plunging off the plateau, dropping several hundred feet.

The trail is slightly challenging as it crosses the outlet of Slide Lake. Difficulty of the crossing depends on the season. During runoff,

The 6-mile hike to Lower Marvine Lake climbs about 1,300 feet.

it may be good to carry lightweight waders so you can stay dry while wading the knee-deep water that runs over the trail. You can rock hop along the outlet side of Slide Lake but this can be tricky when the water is still high. On the downstream side of the trail, from time to time, someone places a log across the stream for a bridge. Don't count on finding one, though, as spring runoff periodically removes it. After runoff, crossing on the rocks at the outlet is easy and you can keep dry without waders then, provided you don't slip.

From Slide Lake, the trail begins climbing faster but still isn't steep. A mile from the stream crossing below Slide Lake, Trail 1823 traverses another creek coming off the high ground to the west. This one is much easier to cross. The small stream is shallow enough to wade if you have waterproof boots, even early in the season. Later in the year, it may be dry, as the stream doesn't run continuously except in very wet years.

The next mile of trail climbs a bit faster but still isn't difficult unless your pack is heavy. You'll pass three small barren ponds on the right before entering the timber again. Three miles farther, the trail rejoins Marvine Creek, which it left above Slide Lake. Just below the creek, there's a wooden gate across the trail, which is no problem for hikers to walk around. At the stream, you'll see a horse trail on the other bank. It connects with the main trail a quarter mile upstream. Hikers, though, can stay on the west bank of the stream, following it through a narrow draw having steep sides along the water. The passage is difficult early in the season—before the snow has melted through here.

A short distance upstream, the trail breaks into the open— beside a quarter-mile-long beaver pond. A couple hundred yards above the pond is a crude log bridge that lets you cross the stream without getting wet. Now, you're almost within sight of Lower Marvine Lake, one of two glacially formed impoundments. For high lakes, they're large; the lower is 65 acres, the upper 88. Fishing in them is good for small brookies and cutthroats. Level campsites are few.

North of Lower Marvine Lake and east of Trail 1823 are two lakes hidden in the pine and spruce forest. The unmarked path is well defined where it leaves Trail 1823 just north of the beaver pond. The hike to Pine Isle is about a half mile. Pine Isle and Ruby Lakes both have fish. There are several good campsites along the shoreline of Pine Isle.

Trail 1823 follows the north shoreline of Lower Marvine Lake. The upper lake is separated from the lower by a string of small, shallow ponds. Along the south end of the lake, you'll see the glacier-piled basalt boulders around the shore that form the dam with the rubble. Lichens growing on the rock indicate many years of exposure. It takes about fifty years for the lichens to get established.

**If you camp here at the beginning of summer,
expect to find snow on the ground.**

One of the area outfitters has a camp established at the upper lake. When you enter the trees along the north shore, you'll find a wooden gate across the trail. Keep it closed so their horses don't wander.

Continuing on Trail 1823 past Upper Marvine Lake, the walls of the glacially carved gorge begin to close in on you. The climb gets a little steeper too. Switchbacks make it less strenuous. You come onto the flat after 5 more miles of hiking, one-half mile north of Trail 1825.

EAST MARVINE TRAIL 1822

UTM 13 0292924 E, 4431577 N
Lat/Lon 40° 00′ 39.12″ N, 107° 25′ 33.69″ W

Description This is a long trail that gives access to the Little Marvine Peaks and Big Marvine Peak and several lakes. The path crosses a large, glacially scoured valley. The wall of ice left the terrain rough and uneven below the nearly vertical walls on the east and south.

Destination Johnson Lake, Trail 1862, Guthrie Lake, Rainbow Lake, Shallow Lake, Mary Loch Lake, Big Marvine Peak Trail, Trail 1825

Distance Johnson Lake 2.25 miles, Trail 1862 2.5 miles, Guthrie Lake 3.9 miles, Rainbow Lake 4.4 miles, Shallow Lake 5 miles, Mary Loch Lake 6 miles, Big Marvine Peak Trail 8.7 miles, Trail 1825 10.3 miles

Elevation 8,081 at trailhead; 11,155 at Big Marvine Peak Trail; 10,989 at Trail 1825

Directions to trailhead From Buford drive 6 miles east on County Road 8, then go right on County Road 12. Cross the bridge on

County Road 12 and head east for 3 miles where the road turns south and follows Marvine Creek. Park at the trailhead. There is also a place to unload horse trailers. The trailhead is 5.5 miles past the bridge over Marvine. The trail begins near the horse corral where it heads generally south. Here you will see a sign and a place to register.

Maps Flat Tops NE

From the trailhead beside the horse corral, you walk down the frequently muddy path to cross the stream. It's big enough that getting to the other side would be a challenge without the bridge. For the first mile, the trail follows the path of East Marvine Creek. The stream is a boisterous, fast moving creek having few quiet pools. In that first mile, you climb 500 feet. You also enter a long narrow valley with open slopes. Straight ahead, to the south, is your first view of the three Little Marvine Peaks. Trail 1822 turns east away from the creek and follows

The three Little Marvine Peaks let you know you're on the right road.

another draw up through the timber past Johnson Lake, which is rumored to have a few lunkers hiding in its shallow waters. By that point, you've gone 2 more miles and ascended another 400 feet.

Johnson Lake sits in a small opening in the forest. The water is clear, the bottom green from the moss. Past the lake, you'll continue your upward path, wandering through dense forest and small, scattered parks. A quarter mile from Johnson Lake, you come to Trail 1862 (1820.1B on USFS map), which leads south to Big Ridge. The junction is 25 yards past a spring that emerges beside the trail. Trail 1822 enters dense forest after crossing a small park a half mile past the junction. At the edge of the trees, you cross a small creek that is challenging early in the year.

A mile farther along Trail 1822, you're into a wet area having several small lakes nearby. Guthrie, Rainbow, and Shallow Lakes are the only ones named. All are reported to have fish. The ground northeast of the trail is hummocky and uneven, left this way at the end of the last ice age. When the glaciers receded, they also left the area pockmarked with many small ponds and lakes. This rough ledge is covered with stands of timber broken by extensive meadows.

A mile up Trail 1822 from Shallow Lake is Mary Loch Lake, hidden from the trail by a small ridge. It is surrounded by timber. The wooded flat on the east side offers level campsites. Shortly before reaching the spur trail, which leads to the lake, the main Trail 1822 again meets Marvine Creek.

Past the Mary Loch Lake spur, you begin seriously climbing now. From the 9,800-foot park northeast of the lake, you climb to 11,000 feet in little more than a mile. Once you climb out, though, the walk is over one of the flattest areas of the Flat Tops. You'll see why the place received its name. The ground is nearly devoid of contours here. Take a look back to the north, where you have a panoramic view of the plateau and the Little Marvine Peaks. Four miles to the east, you'll see Trappers Peak and Big Marvine rises abruptly in front of you to the southwest.

A mile past the top of the canyon, you come to Trail 1822.2A leading to the summit of Big Marvine Peak. This mile-and-a-half detour takes you to one of the higher points on the Flat Tops at 11,879 feet.

One and one-half miles past the detour, you arrive at the junction of Trail 1825, a quarter mile west of Twin Lakes.

BIG MARVINE PEAK TRAIL 1822.2A

UTM 13 0302297 E, 4425391 N
Lat/Lon 39° 57' 27.10" N, 107° 18' 52.25" W

Description A side trip here gives hikers a magnificent vista of the wilderness and surrounding area.

This trail takes you to the top of Big Marvine Peak, a prominent feature of the Flat Tops Wilderness.

Destination Big Marvine Peak summit

Distance 2 miles

Elevation 11,155 at junction with Trail 1822; 11,879 on Big Marvine Peak

Directions to trail Eight miles from East Marvine Creek Trailhead, 2 miles from Trail 1825

Big Marvine Peak is visible from many vantage points. The mountain was one of several volcanic vents that extruded lava only a few million years ago, or perhaps a bit more recently. It's one bit of evidence of the relatively young age of the Flat Tops Plateau.

The east half of the peak appears rather solid, in contrast with the western flank, which is covered with rubble from slides. Big Marvine is a typical mountain of this wilderness, being massive but rising less than 1,000 feet above the plateau. It's not the height, though, that's impressive as much as the massiveness of the block of basalt that forms the peak.

After crossing the plateau from Trail 1822, the route up the peak (Trail 1822.2A) ascends the steep east slope, the climb made somewhat easier by the switchbacks. On top, you will be able to appreciate the vastness of the wilderness as you scan the plateau. Return to Trail 1822 to continue hiking south to the plateau.

Maps Flat Tops NE

BIG RIDGE TRAIL 1820

UTM 13 0287946 E, 4434811 N
Lat/Lon 40° 2' 19.59" N, 107° 29' 7.45" W

Description The trail follows a feature known as Big Ridge. The first 3 miles are a steady climb. Once on the ridge, parks are interspersed among the timber. Only the last mile of the trail lies within the wilderness. This trail is popular for horse trips from the nearby lodges.

Destination Trail 1820.1B, Sable Lake, Trail 1821

Distance 5 miles to Trail 1820.1B, 10 miles to Sable Lake, 13 miles to Trail 1821

Elevation 7,550 at trailhead; 10,161 east of Sable Lake; 9,936 at Trail 1821

Directions to trailhead From Buford drive 6 miles east on County Road 8, then go right on County Road 12. Cross the bridge on County Road 12 and head east for 3 miles where the road turns south. Here the trailhead is marked to show Big Ridge Trail 1820. It is next to a sign for Lost Creek Outfitters. Parking is limited with space for two or three cars.

Maps Flat Tops NE

The trail starts climbing at the parking lot, following the nose of Big Ridge for nearly 5 miles to Big Park. In this distance, you walk through heavy timber and scattered open meadows. The climb flattens across Big Park, where you come to the junction of Wild Cow Park Trail 1820.1B.

The next 2 miles wander through Big Park, a broad meadow having a scattering of timber. The Big Ridge Trail then begins a second ascent that takes you to Sable Lake, 10 miles from your starting point.

Pack plenty of water as there is no reliable source between the trailhead and the lake. The wooded land is nearly flat north and east of the lake, making it a good choice for a campsite. Sable Lake is a small lake with an east-west orientation. It sits on a shelf below Sable Point, a near-vertical wall 1 mile south of the lake. Sable Point is a prominent landmark, seen from other areas of the north side of the wilderness. The lake has large cutthroats that can be picky about what they eat and when they eat it.

Going east from Sable Lake, Trail 1820 climbs less than 200 feet before beginning a gradual descent to Trail 1821, 3 miles past Sable

The trail heads up the ridge to the right.
The road on the left is private.

Lake. Trail 1820 joins the Mirror Lake Trail a half mile east of Mirror Lake in an opening along the nose of a small ridge.

If your destination is Sable Lake, the hike will be shorter by coming in on Trail 1821, the Mirror Lake Trail. The junction is marked with a sign reading "Big Ridge Trail."

Some older maps show Trail 1820 descending a steep slope using switchbacks to connect with Trail 1821. This portion is no longer maintained as downed timber on the trail has not been cleared for several years. You can still hike it but the going will be rough.

WILD COW PARK TRAIL 1820.1B

BIG RIDGE TRAIL JUNCTION
UTM 13 294399 E, 4434260 N
Lat/Lon 40° 2' 9.86" N, 107° 24' 34.52" W

EAST MARVINE TRAIL JUNCTION
UTM 13 296264 E, 4430921 N
Lat/Lon 40° 0′ 20.68″ N, 107° 23′ 12.20″ W

Description This is a short connecting trail that has little change in elevation. There's no water along this route.

Destination Connects Trails 1820 and 1822

Distance 3 miles

Elevation 9,570 at Trail 1820; 9,480 at Trail 1822

Directions to trail From Buford drive 6 miles east on County Road 8, then go right on County Road 12. Cross the bridge on County Road 12 and head east for 3 miles where the road turns south. Five miles east on Trail 1820 or 3 miles east on Trail 1822.

The south end of Trail 1862 can be accessed from Trail 1822. On County Road 12 head east for 3 miles where the road turns south and follows Marvine Creek. Park at the East Marvine Creek Trailhead. There is also a place to unload horses and park trailers. The trailhead is 5.5 miles past the bridge over Marvine. The trail begins near the horse corral where it heads generally south. Here you will see a sign and a place to register.

Maps Flat Tops NE

This trail heads south 5 miles east of the Big Ridge Trailhead. It crosses the west end of Big Park Creek. The first 2 miles take you through open parks and the edges of stands of timber. Elevation changes are moderate, making the stroll pleasant. After another 2 miles, you enter the wilderness. From here to Trail 1822, the ground is hummocky, the result of having glaciers do the landscaping. You connect with Trail 1862 a short distance east of Johnson Lake, the first source of water since leaving the Big Ridge Trailhead.

Trail 1820.1B does not appear on the USGS Lost Park quad. It's listed on the 1991 White River National Forest map as Trail 1820.1B and on the Trails Illustrated map as Trail 1862.

BIG RIDGE CUTOFF TRAIL 1820.1A

Trailhead
UTM 13 289639E, 4436120 N
Lat/Lon 40° 3' 3.43" N, 107° 27' 59.37" W

Big Ridge Trail Junction
UTM 13 291591 E, 4434473 N
Lat/Lon 40 2' 10.74" N. 107° 26" 33.65" W

Description This trail is an alternate route to Trail 1820 and Big Ridge. The trailhead is on private land and may not be accessible without permission from the landowner. The forest boundary is about 0.1 mile south of the river. From this point, the trail ascends the steep north slope of Big Ridge, climbing 600 feet before leveling out some. The trail swings eastward, still climbing but not so severely. After crossing the slope, it turns south again and ascends to Big Ridge.

Destination Trail 1820

Distance 2 miles

Elevation 7,599 at County Road 8; 9,030 at Trail 1820

Directions to trailhead From Buford drive 12 miles east on County Road 8, then, 0.1 mile past the Lost Creek Guard Station. The trail is south of County Road 8.

Maps Flat Tops NE

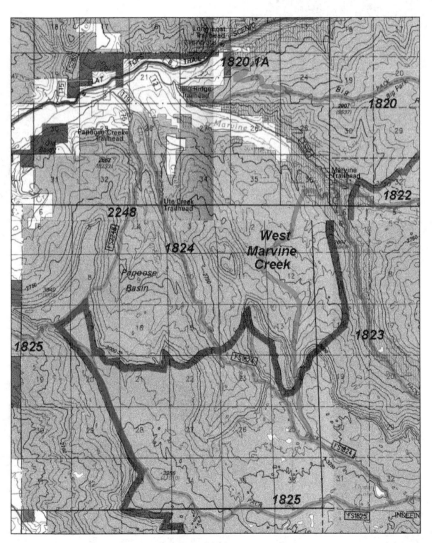

PAPOOSE BASIN

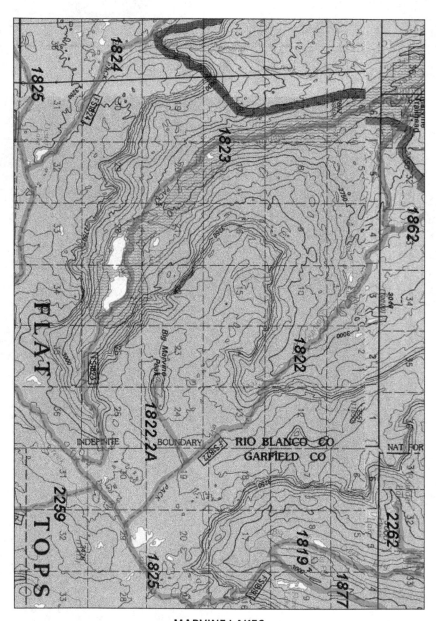

MARVINE LAKES

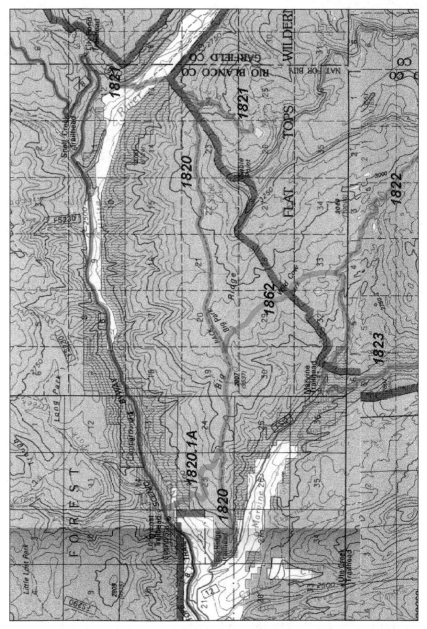

MARVINE CREEK

6

FOREST ROAD 205 (TRAPPERS LAKE ROAD)

Forest Road 205 17 miles east of Buford goes south, ending at Trappers Lake. The road gives access to Forest Road 206, Picket Pin Trail Head, Himes Peak Campground, Skinny Fish Trail Head, Trappers Lake Lodge, Trappers Outlet Trail Head, Trappers Lake campgrounds, and Wall Lake and Scotts Bay Trailheads.

MIRROR LAKE TRAIL 1821

TRAILHEAD
UTM 13 0301807 E, 4437070 N
Lat/Lon 40° 3' 45.57" N, 107° 19' 25.70 W

BIG RIDGE TRAIL JUNCTION
UTM 13 0301243 E, 4434763 N
Lat/Lon 40° 2' 29.58" N, 107° 19' 47.07" W

Description The trail has several steep sections, made easier by switchbacks. Mirror Lake is close enough to do the round-trip in a day without rushing. This is a popular route for trail rides.

Destination Trail 1820, Shamrock Lake, Mirror Lake, Sable Lake

Distance 3 miles to Trail 1820, 3.5 miles to Shamrock Lake, 4 miles to Mirror Lake, 5 miles to Sable Lake

Elevation 8,380 at trailhead; 10,040 at Mirror Lake

Directions to trailhead Beginning at Forest Road 8, beside Ripple Creek drive south on Forest Road 205 0.3 mile to junction with Forest Road 206. Turn west on Forest Road 206. The trailhead and parking area is at the end of Forest Road 206 about 0.25 mile from Forest Road 205 (Trappers Lake Road).

Maps Flat Tops NE

The trail leads the hiker down a gentle incline through an open meadow on the way to the North Fork of the White River. A quarter mile from the trailhead, the path goes through a gate onto private land owned by the Rio Blanco Ranch. Stay on the trail as numerous signs warn of severe consequences for straying. Also, watch for cattle that graze in the meadow. Remember to respect private property.

After crossing a wooden bridge, the trail begins to climb. A short distance farther, you enter the coniferous forest and the wilderness. Make certain to close the gate at the boundary to prevent cattle from gaining access to the wooded grassland they would love to devour and spoil with massive calling cards.

While the trail to Mirror Lake is a constant climb, the grade is not difficult. The few steep sections use switchbacks to make the walk easier. The trees shade most of the narrow path, making the stroll pleasant, especially on warm, dry days.

After a nearly 4-mile hike, you will enter a small clearing. To the southwest, below the path, lies Shamrock Lake, so named because of the translucent green color of the water. Pause a few moments to watch the numerous 8- and 10-inch brook trout enjoy a meal of insects they find on the lake's surface, some exuberantly jumping out of the

The trail begins on the Rio Blanco Ranch, which is privately owned. To avoid trespassing stay on the trail until reaching the wilderness boundary.

water as they feed. The angling hiker or rider may be tempted to rig up a fly rod. Try a small, dark-colored pattern.

A mile past Shamrock Lake, you come to the junction of Trail 1820. A sign reading "Big Ridge Trail" marks the junction. Continue southwest through the junction to stay on Trail 1821. Now, you have only two more small rises to cross before reaching your destination. Your first view of Mirror Lake comes as you cross the last low rise. Ideally, the sky will be clear, the wind calm, showing a perfect reflection of the nearly vertical 1,400-foot wall standing along the lake's southwest margin. This is the time to pause, remove your pack, and dig out a camera. Then sit awhile and enjoy the scene.

Again, the angler will be induced to make an effort to catch a few of the many small brookies seen swimming along the shoreline. They're susceptible to both lures and flies. A few appear emaciated but most are fat and sassy and eager to take a Rio Grande King or other fly of your choice.

The majority of Mirror Lake's shoreline is open and it's easy to circumnavigate the crude path around it. This trail can be done as a day hike but for an overnighter you'll find a level meadow to camp east of the lake and south of the trail.

On the east side of Mirror Lake, an abandoned but still visible trail heads east toward Paradise Creek. It descends gradually for the first mile and a half, and then follows sharp switchbacks to descend to the creek. It follows the stream down to the confluence with the North Fork of the White River. Be aware, though, that if you take this route, you will be on the Rio Blanco Ranch when you leave the wilderness. This area of the ranch is not open for public use so you may want to avoid using the Paradise Creek Trail.

BIG FISH TRAIL 1819

UTM 13 0306214 E, 4433087 N
Lat/Lon 40° 1′ 39.03″ N, 107° 16′ 15.21″ W

Description This is an especially scenic trail. It follows Big Fish Creek up a broad U-shaped valley. Don't forget your camera on this hike. If you enjoy horses, this is a good trail to ride.

Destination Trail 2262, Big Fish Lake, Trail 1877, Trail 1825

Distance 2 miles to Trail 2262, 4 miles to Big Fish Lake, 5 miles to Trail 1877, 7 miles to Trail 1825

Elevation 8,780 at trailhead; 10,930 at junction of Trail 1825

Directions to trailhead From Buford drive 17 miles east on County

Road 8 (Forest Road 8 past USFS boundary), go south on Forest Road 205 4.4 miles to Himes Peak Campground. Park near the trailhead at the north end of the campground by the horse unloading area.

Maps Flat Tops NE

During the summer of 2002, over 23,000 acres of the White River and Routt National Forests were burned by the lightning-caused Big Fish and Lost Lakes Fires. These fires affected areas surrounding Trappers Lake and to the immediate north of both East and West Lost Lakes. Access to the fire area is not limited and all trails are open. Some areas in the Flat Tops Wilderness, however, may present hazardous situations for backcountry travelers. Please read and adhere to the recommendations below before entering the wilderness.

Some trail material is unstable and subject to erosion. Whether hiking or traveling with horses and pack stock, exercise extreme caution when using trails in the burned area. Even gentle winds can bring down dead, standing trees or "snags." Select campsites that are at least tree-length distances away from hazardous, burned, or unstable trees.

The fire also loosened rocks, boulders, and other materials on slopes located in the burn area. It is not uncommon for loose objects to become dislodged and suddenly roll downhill onto trails. Use caution and remain alert while traveling along or below burned hillsides.

Remain aware of your surroundings and use plenty of common sense when traveling and camping in the Flat Tops Wilderness. Hazards remaining from the fire will be present for many years and can cause serious injury or death. Be safe.

The drive south along the North Fork gives a view of the Big Fish burn. The extent of the Big Fish fire is visible from the road.

Park at the Himes Peak Campground in the shadow of Himes

The fire burned several thousand acres of dead timber in 2002.

Peak, which is 2 miles to the south. This prominent landmark reaches a height of 11,201 feet. As you hike the trail, you will rarely stray from sight of this peak.

After departing the campground, you follow a meandering trail down to the North Fork of the White River, which is little more than a creek in size here. On the other side of the stream, the trail begins a gradual climb, paralleling Big Fish Creek. The junction of Trail 2262, which leads to Boulder Lake, is 2 miles from the trailhead. While you walk on Trail 1819 through the meadow above the junction, look to the left, to the slope south of Himes Peak to catch a view of Bessies Falls.

In the first 4 miles of your hike, you stroll through a mix of timber, open meadows, and willows on the way to Big Fish Lake. The lake is stocked with rainbows averaging 10 inches in length.

Campsite choices leave much to be desired. There are small flat spots around Big Fish Lake but they're close to the trail. The ground at the north and south ends of the lake is level but in the open. The timber on the west side could be your best choice.

A mile above Big Fish Lake, a crude unmarked trail leads to Gwendolyn Lake. Gwendolyn Lake is hidden among the trees on a small ledge a mile south of Big Fish Lake and is reported to have cutthroats.

After passing the junction, Trail 1819 wanders along the edge of a large meadow before entering the timber and beginning a serious climb. A mile or so past Big Fish Lake, you encounter a single long switchback.

Along the switchback, you connect with Trail 1877, which heads off to the northeast, uphill through the trees. Trail 1877 leads to Florence Lake and around the north side of Himes Peak. You'll find campsites along the lake. It's said the lake is fishless.

Another mile along Trail 1819, beyond the junction with Trail 1877, takes you to a steep, heart-pounding climb. You'll go from 10,200 to 10,760 within one-half mile. And while it may be repetitious, it's just another mile up a slight rise to the flat and Trail 1825.

BOULDER LAKE TRAIL 2262

UTM 13 305452 E, 4431474 N
Lat/Lon 40° 0' 46.75 N, 107° 16' 45.73" W

Description This trail takes you up a pretty good climb, but the emerald green lake at the end makes it worth the effort.

Destination Boulder Lake

Distance 2.5 miles

Elevation 8,930 at Trail 1819; 9,770 at Boulder Lake

Directions to trail From Forest Road 8 at the junction of Forest Road 205, go south to Himes Peak Campground. Begin at the Trail 1819 Trailhead at Himes Peak Campground. Hike 2 miles along Trail 1819 to the junction with Boulder Lake Trail 2262.

Maps Flat Tops NE

The trail takes off to the west from Trail 1819 at the edge of a sloping meadow. You descend a short distance to cross Big Fish Creek, and then begin climbing. The hill is steep but switchbacks moderate the grade as you ascend.

After a 2-mile walk, you come out of the timber onto a large flat opening. Through the middle of the clearing is the small stream flowing out of Boulder Lake. You first see the lake from above. The clear water appears green from the mossy bottom. The lake may be barren following the Big Fish Fire of 2002. The ground is flat enough on the north and south sides for camping. Watch for elk in this area.

Less than a mile south of Boulder Lake is Doris Lake. No trail leads to it, but by following the meadow east of Boulder Lake up the moderately steep slope, and following the contour around the nose of the timbered ridge, you should find it. The best campsite is probably the meadow south of Doris Lake. Be sure to stay well back from the water.

LAKE OF THE WOODS TRAIL 2263

UTM 13 308152 E, 4431987 N
Lat/Lon 40° 1′ 5.12 ″ N, 107° 14′ 52.81″ W

Description This trail creates additional hiking opportunities near the Trappers Lake Campground. It's an easy walk to get you adjusted to the altitude. Tall spruce and pines that burned in a lightning-caused fire in 2002 surround Lake of the Woods. Until the fire, the lake was not visible from the road. Fireweed, the tall pink flower, covers the ground among the burned-out pines. Hikers may also find rare red columbines here. The lake has brookies up to 16 inches.

Destination Trail 2261, Lake of the Woods

Distance 0.25 mile to Trail 2261, 0.5 mile to Lake of the Woods

Elevation 9,250 at Forest Road 205; 9,010 at Lake of the Woods

Directions to trailhead From County Road 8 (Forest Road 8), go south 6.7 miles on Forest Road 205 to Trail 2263. Park beside the road by the sign for Lake of the Woods. You'll often see other cars parked here.

Maps Flat Tops NE

This photo was taken four years after the Big Fish Fire, illustrating how quickly the land recovers.

DUCK LAKE TRAIL 2261

UTM 13 308510 E, 4429267N
Lat/Lon 39° 59' 37.87" N, 107° 14' 34.19 W

Description This is one of several trails accessed near Trappers Lake Campground. It connects a bike path out of the campground with Trail 2263. A short and very easy walk.

Destination Lake of the Woods Trail 2263

Distance 1 mile

Elevation 9,520 at bike path; 9,240 at Trail 2263

Directions to trailhead From Buford drive 17 miles east on County Road 8, go south 7.8 miles on Forest Road 205 to Forest Road 209, then 1.25 miles to Trappers Lake Campground. Park at the overflow area and hike south on the Duck Lake Trail.

Maps Flat Tops NE

The trail goes north through the timber and loops around east to connect with Forest Road 209. This trail is open to bicycles.

HIMES PEAK TRAIL 1877

UTM 13 308514 E, 4429272 N
Lat/Lon 39° 59' 31.08" N, 107° 14' 36.61" W

Description This trail takes you around the north side of Himes Peak and along Florence Lake. It was constructed in 1993.

Destination Florence Lake, Trail 1819

Distance 4 miles to Florence Lake, 5 miles to Trail 1819

Elevation 9,755 at Wall Lake Trailhead; 10,400 west of Himes Peak

Directions to trailhead From County Road 8, go south 8 miles on Forest Road 205 to Trappers Lake Lodge across the road east of Forest Road 205. Forest Road 209 goes southwest across the North Fork of the White River, across from the lodge. It's 1.25 miles to the campground. Continue west to the turn south and park along the road by the trail sign.

Maps Flat Tops NE

This recently completed trail takes you on a walk around the north side of Himes Peak. It begins near the Wall Lake Trailhead and leads west up a moderate slope of pine forest and open, marshy meadows. After a half-mile hike, it turns north to go around the base of the peak, which rises to a height of 11,201 feet. This is a prominent landmark you'll see for some distance along the road on the way to begin your walk.

The grade is moderate as the trail rounds the peak, and then turns southwest. As you come closer to the side of the mountain, the path becomes steeper and uses switchbacks to make a short descent. A little farther along, the path flattens, leading onto a long, narrow, open shelf holding picturesque Florence Lake. If you plan to camp, you'll find sites on the level ground west and south of the lake, well away from the water. There are no fish in the lake but the scenery makes the walk or horse ride worthwhile.

Past Florence Lake, the trail continues southwest through the timber, where it soon joins Trail 1819 after a half-mile hike. From here hikers have a couple of options for the return trip. Trail 1819 leads downhill past Big Fish Lake and ends at Himes Peak Campground, a distance of about 8 miles. The second option is to hike 2 miles south on Trail 1819 to the junction of Trail 1825, and then follow it east 1 mile to the Wall Lake Trail 1818. Go north on Trail 1818, which descends to the Scotts Bay Trailhead, about 3.5 miles.

Trappers Lake

Not only is Trappers Lake one of the better known landmarks on the Flat Tops, it is also the largest natural body of water in the wilderness. It has

Himes Peak is a prominent landmark along the road to Trappers Lake.

an area of 320 acres and is reported to have a depth of 180 feet. Trappers was created when a wall of ice piled rubble across the north end of the basin, forming a natural dam. It is believed that this occurred at the close of the Wisconsin period, the final episode of glaciation in North America that ended a few thousand years ago. Rock to form the dam came from carving the Chinese Wall and the valleys leading into the basin. The lake is the source of the North Fork of the White River.

Trappers has long been famous for its nearly pure strain of Colorado River cutthroat trout. In spite of the pressure it receives, it's still a good fishery. This is due in part to special regulations for the lake. The use of bait is prohibited. Anglers are restricted to using flies or lures only and all fish over 11 inches must be released unharmed. Certain areas of the lake, such as inlet streams and the outlet, are off-limits to anglers. This protects the breeding size fish.

In the spring, the cutthroats make spawning runs up the inlet streams around the lake. Colorado Division of Wildlife biologists net

Trappers Lake is the origin of the North Fork of the White River.

View of Trappers Lake from the Scotts Bay Trailhead.

the fish as they try to spawn to collect the eggs for hatchery operations. Division personnel use the cabins you see on the east shore during this operation. The Colorado River cutthroat is considered a threatened species and rearing in the CPW's hatcheries is one way the species is being protected.

In recent years, brook trout have made their way into Trappers Lake. Because they are so prolific, soon overpopulating a lake or pond, they compete for food with the native cutthroat trout. As such, CPW has no restrictions on brookies other than method of angling. Fishermen are encouraged to remove all brook trout caught and not return them to the lake.

Because Trappers is within the wilderness, the use of motorized equipment is prohibited. That doesn't mean you can't get out on the lake, though. Hand-propelled boats are allowed, as are belly boats. Trappers Lake Lodge & Resort rents rowboats and canoes, which are kept along the northeast shoreline. Make arrangements for rentals at

A float tube hatch typically occurs on Trappers Lake each year around Memorial Day.

the lodge office. If you're not familiar with the lake or fishing it, you can hire a guide through the lodge.

Not everyone who visits Trappers comes for the fishing. The scenic beauty alone makes it worth the trip. For the non-angler, there's still an opportunity to watch these colorful trout. The outlet stream is an especially good place to observe them in the evenings as they rise to tiny insects on the surface or scrounge for nymphs on the bottom of the clear stream. Watch the sky as an occasional osprey may make an appearance as it searches for a meal of trout.

To help preserve the wilderness environment around the lake, camping is prohibited within a quarter mile of the shoreline. Campgrounds are provided, though, on the northwest side of Trappers Lake and are accessible by cars, trailers, and RVs.

WALL LAKE TRAIL 1818

UTM 13 0308543 E, 4428974 N
Lat/Lon 39° 59' 27.90" N, 107° 14' 33.29" W

Description The ascent on this trail is deceptive. It's a continuous climb, but the grade is never steep until you get near the headwall of the unnamed creek that feeds into Trappers Lake. You get a very good view of Trappers Lake along the trail as you ascend the valley and again near Wall Lake at a place named the Amphitheatre. Once on top, the trail is nearly flat as it meanders over tundra and through scattered patches of timber.

Destination Trail 1825, Wall Lake, Trail 1816

Distance 2.5 miles to Trail 1825, 4 miles to Wall Lake, 7 miles to Trail 1816

Elevation 9,755 at Trailhead; 11,190 south of Wall Lake

Directions to trailhead From County Road 8, go south 8 miles on Forest Road 205 to Trappers Lake Lodge across the road east of Forest Road 205. Forest Road 209 goes southwest across the North Fork of the White River, across from the lodge. It's 1.7 miles from the turnoff to the Wall Lake Trailhead, just past the turn to Scotts Bay Trailhead.

Maps Flat Tops NE

As you leave the parking lot the trail begins on a southwest bearing and you immediately enter burned stands of spruce and lodgepole pine, the result of the 2002 Big Fish Fire. This trail is one of the quickest but steepest routes up to the plateau. A half mile from the trailhead, on the east side of the trail, you'll see two off-colored mosquito hatcheries. Take along some DEET and use it liberally, especially early in the season. A little farther, you pass Anderson Lake, again on the left. A few yards past the lake, the trail crosses a sloping meadow, where you have your first view of the vertical walls at the top of the valley. About halfway up the trail, you'll have a good view of Trappers Lake, off to the east.

Though it doesn't show on the topos, several snowmelt streams cross the trail, providing adequate water for your hike. About 3 miles from the trailhead, the ascent begins climbing faster up the side of this cirque carved during the last ice age. Switchbacks make it bearable. Just keep in mind that in 4 miles, you climb nearly 2,300 feet.

As you approach the top of the valley, look to the left. There, the stream that drains the pothole lakes at the rim plunges over several falls at the headwall, dropping nearly vertically for 200 feet. It's worth a photo.

The last few feet of your climb take you across the steep, rocky slope of the headwall. Once on top, you can look back down the deep valley and think, "Hey, that wasn't so bad."

As soon as you top out on the plateau, you reach the junction with Trail 1825. Trail 1818 leads to the south, 1825 to the west. The junction is marked only with a post and it is easy to miss the connecting trail, as it's almost obscured by low willows.

Heading southeast toward Wall Lake along Trail 1818, you pass four unnamed pothole lakes sitting on the open tundra below Trappers Peak. The massive peak rises a thousand feet above the land to an elevation of 12,002. The trail south crosses low rises in the treeless plain. Scattered patches of low willows are the only growth for nearly a mile. The trail along this area is across easily eroded land. Over the

The trail climbs about 1,100 feet from the trailhead to the rim.

years, several parallel paths have created a scar, illustrating graphically the need to stay on established routes.

Wall Lake is 2 miles past the canyon rim. It sits out in the open on a flat overlooking a cirque named the Amphitheatre. In the distance across the valley is the Chinese Wall and a section of the plateau that extends for several miles north. Trappers Lake can be seen in the distance. Good campsites can be found in the timber near Wall Lake.

A half mile past Wall Lake, the trail crosses a low, barely discernible pass, the high point on the trail. In the next mile, you descend no more than 100 feet as you cross a large flat covered with the remnants of the ice age. Pothole lakes and marshes cover the area. On the open flat, you connect with an abandoned trail that wanders west for a mile above the South Fork Canyon. Trail 1818 works its way around the head of the canyon, where it connects with Trail 1816.

As you approach Trail 1816, you cross several tiny trickles forming the headwaters of the South Fork of the White River, flowing nearly a thousand feet below the soles of your hiking boots.

Trappers Peak, 12,002 feet, is your first view on reaching the plateau.

At the junction with Trail 1816 hikers and those riding horses have a few options for a return trip, or for exploring other parts of the Flat Tops. Going north on Trail 1816 leads to Trappers Lake. Heading south on Trail 1816 takes you to Indian Camp Pass close to Forest Road 600. As is seen on the National Geographic Trails Illustrated Flat Tops NE map, the possibilities for extended trips are many.

STILLWATER TRAIL 1814

UTM 13 0309617 E, 4429843 N
Lat/Lon 39° 59′ 56.94″ N, 107° 13′ 48.48″ W

Description This one takes you on a steep hike up the Chinese Wall to the top of the plateau, where you connect with other trails. Trail 1120, to the east, takes you into the Bear River drainage and to Still-water Trailhead.

Destination Trail 1815, Coffin Lake, Little Trappers Lake, Surprise Lake Trail, Trail 1803, Trail 1120

Distance 1 mile to Trail 1815, 1.5 miles to Coffin Lake, 2 miles to Little Trappers Lake, 4 miles to Surprise Lake Trail, 5 miles to Trail 1803, 5.3 miles to Trail 1120

Elevation 9,690 at trailhead; 11,314 at Trail 1803

Directions to trail From the junction of Forest Roads 205 and 209, drive south a quarter mile to the Outlet Trailhead parking area, follow Trail 1815 south three-quarters of a mile along the east shoreline to Colorado Parks and Wildlife (CPW) cabins. Stillwater Trail 1814 heads east from Trappers Lake.

Maps Flat Tops NE

The wall beside the parking lot for the Outlet Trailhead is a part of the moraine that dammed Trappers Lake. Your hike begins by ascending this low remnant of glacial rubble.

When you reach the outlet of Trappers Lake a quarter mile from the Outlet Trailhead, continue around the east shoreline. Between the trail and shoreline, you'll see two cabins to the south. They were built about a century ago and the Colorado Parks and Wildlife now uses them as their base of operations during the spring when cutthroats are spawning. The Trappers Lake cutts supply CPW with most of the spawn used in their hatcheries.

Near the cabins is the junction of Trail 1815, which takes you on a 5-mile stroll around Trappers Lake. Heading east up Trail 1814 by the CPW cabins leads past Coffin and Little Trappers Lakes. The climb is noticeable but not strenuous. Coffin Lake sits secluded in a small basin, timbered on one side and the other being a steeply piled remnant of rubble discarded by a passing glacier. The water appears dark, even

**Rare red columbines can be found in a few places in the Flat Tops.
Look for them along this trail in shady areas.**

lifeless. Don't let that fool you, though, as it's reported that the CPW sometimes stocks old brood fish of such a size as to create fish stories.

After leaving Coffin Lake, the trail winds its way up the steep-sided, narrow canyon of the stream draining Little Trappers. The walk is not difficult as the ascent is moderate and steady. Not quite a mile from Coffin Lake, the trail breaks out into the open on a shelf holding Little Trappers Lake. The lake sits below a steep, timbered hillside that rises more than 1,000 feet to the south. You have a view of the southern end of the Chinese Wall, which is a mile to the east. Little Trappers is small and not too deep. Its cutthroats are small, about 10 to 13 inches and anxious to take a fly. If you plan to stay overnight, you can find campsites in the open flat east of the lake or in the wooded area to the north.

Past Little Trappers, the trail again climbs, leading across the lower slopes of the Chinese Wall before making the ascent up the seemingly vertical rock face. Switchbacks make the upward hike bearable. After 2 miles of climbing, you break out on the plateau 1,100 feet above the lake. You come to the abandoned trail that leads to Surprise Lake a half mile west of the Chinese Wall and 2 miles south from Trail 1814. Another half mile past the Surprise Lake trail takes you to the junction of Trails 1803 and 1120.

At this junction you can take the Chinese Wall Trail 1803 north 8 miles to a connection with Trail 1812. Follow Trail 1812 south 3 miles to the Skinny Fish Trailhead.

Continuing east on Trail 1803 a quarter mile you come to the Bear River Trail 1120 in Routt National Forest. This leads west past a few lakes to fish. Trail 1120 ends at the east end of Stillwater Reservoir, a total hike of 4 miles from the junction with Trail 1803. The Flat Tops NE map shows other possibilities for an extended hike or horse trip.

CARHART TRAIL 1815

UTM 13 0309617 E, 4429843 N
Lat/Lon 39° 59′ 56.94″ N, 107° 13′ 48.48″ W

Description This trail takes you on a loop trip as it follows close to the shoreline of Trappers Lake.

Destination Trappers Lake Loop

Distance 5.6 miles

Elevation 9,590 at Forest Road 205; 11,275 on the plateau above Fraser Creek

Directions to trailhead From the junction of Forest Roads 205 and 209, drive south a quarter mile to the Outlet Trailhead parking area.

Trappers Lake is the crown jewel of the Flat Tops Wilderness Area. Arthur Carhart, for whom this trail is named, believed the area was too valuable a resource to allow development to occur here. It was his dream that culminated in the Wilderness Act of 1964, saving the Flat Tops for future generations. A plaque along the lake trail honors this visionary conservationist.

Begin at the Outlet Trailhead and walk south along the east shoreline on Trail 1814. Past the Colorado Parks and Wildlife cabins, the trail connects to Trail 1815 and continues south, taking you over the open shoreline of the lake. High above you to the southeast lies the Chinese Wall, rising vertically nearly 2,000 feet and nearly surrounding the lake. A mile past the Outlet Trailhead, Trail 1814 goes east to the Chinese Wall.

From this junction by the CPW cabins, Trail 1815 heads south past the east shoreline. Follow the trail about 1.4 miles to the junction of Trail 1816. Here Trail 1815 heads west along the edge of a meadow to cross Fraser Creek, one of the inlet streams that supplies Trappers. After crossing the creek, the trail climbs a bit through the trees, where it crosses a stream flowing down through the Amphitheatre.

The trail turns northeast and leads across a timbered slope before emerging into a large meadow having several small ponds. You cross another unnamed creek feeding the lake and come to a T-junction. Going left takes you to Wall Lake Trail 1818; turning north on Trail 1815 leads back to the Trappers Lake shoreline. You can follow the shore to connect with the Scotts Lake Trail and return to the Outlet Trailhead. At the north end of Trappers Lake, you cross the outlet stream. No fishing is allowed here. This is a good place to watch the native cutthroat in the clear water below the bridge as they rise to feed on the many insects at the surface.

SURPRISE LAKE TRAIL (ABANDONED)

UTM 13 313910 E, 4429000 N
Lat/Lon 39° 59′ 32.81 N, 107° 10′ 47.34 W

Description This route is more a game trail than hiking trail. It is not maintained and is difficult to follow. You will find it marked on the Trails Illustrated Flat Tops NE Trappers Lake map. The above-timberline route follows the edge of the plateau from the Chinese Wall south to Trail 1803.

Destination Surprise Lake, Trail 1803

Distance 2 miles to Surprise Lake; 3.5 miles to Trail 1803

Elevation 11,150 at Trail 1814; 11,520 at Trail 1803

Directions to trail From the CPW cabins by Trappers Lake, hike almost 4 four miles east along Trail 1814. The trail to Surprise Lake is abandoned and not marked.

Maps Flat Tops NE

Surprise Lake is reported to have cutthroat trout.

TRAPPERS LAKE TRAIL 1816

UTM 13 0310336 E, 4427053 N
Lat/Lon 39° 58′ 26.59 N, 107° 13′ 15.74″ W

Description This trail takes you cross country from north to south across the plateau.

Destination Parvin Lake, Trail 1842 , Trail 1818, 1832 Trail, Rim Lake and Trail 1856, Shepherd Lake, Indian Lake, Indian Camp Pass

Distance 3 miles to Parvin Lake, 5 miles to Trail 1842, 6.7 miles to Trail 1818, 9 miles to Trail 1832, 11 miles to Rim Lake and Trail 1856, 12 miles to Shepherd Lake, 14 miles to Indian Lake, 16 miles to Indian Camp Pass

Elevation 9,908 at Trail 1815; 11,275 on the plateau above Fraser Creek; 9,724 at Indian Camp Pass

Directions to trail Ten miles south of Rio Blanco County Road 8 on Forest Road 205 (Trappers Lake Road), 0.25 mile north of Trappers Lake. Park at the Outlet Trailhead. Take Trail 1814 0.8 mile along east shoreline of Trappers Lake to junction of Trail 1815. Hike 1.5 miles south on Trail 1815 to junction with Trail 1816.

Maps Flat Tops NE

Park at the Outlet Trailhead and hike south on Trail 1814 along the east side of Trappers Lake. At the CPW cabins go south on Trail 1815 1.5 miles and continue south on Trail 1816 past Parvin Lake. The trail climbs about 700 feet past Parvin Lake to the junction of Trail 1817 on the plateau. Continue south on Trail 1816, which goes along the west side of Shingle Peak on the way 3.7 miles to the junction with Trail 1832. Here hikers have the option to go east to Crescent and Mackinaw Lakes.

The hike is easy after reaching the plateau above Parvin Lake all the way to the wall above the Indian Camp Trailhead, a distance of nearly 9 miles. The elevation change is only about 600 feet. The ground is open giving a view of most of the wilderness high points.

At the junction of Trails 1816 and 1856 you can see Rim Lake. It sits at the head of the canyon drained by Sweetwater Creek and is the stream's source. It's out in the open. The tallest vegetation around it is the willows that crowd the shoreline in places.

A mile past Rim Lake you come to Shepherd Lake a short distance north of the trail. You pass a few pothole lakes as you hike south to Indian Lake, 3 miles from the end of your hike. The Indian Camp Trailhead is about 800 feet below at the end of your descent.

For details of this trail see the description of Trail 1816 starting at Indian Camp Pass.

SKINNY FISH TRAIL 1813

UTM 13 0309036 E, 4431754 N
Lat/Lon 40° 00′ 58.77″ N, 107° 14′ 15.30 W

Description The trail has a few steep sections in the first mile but the climb isn't bad. It follows Skinny Fish Creek for most of the way. At the lakes, you are surrounded by the Chinese Wall. Beautiful setting with good campsites.

Destination Trail 1812, Skinny Fish and McGinnis Lakes

Distance 1 mile to Trail 1813; 2.7 miles to Skinny Fish and McGinnis Lakes

Elevation 9,235 at trailhead; 10,192 at Skinny Fish Lake

Directions to trailhead From Buford drive 17 miles east of County Road 8, go south 6.7 miles on Forest Road 205. The trailhead is on the east side of the road by Skinny Fish Creek, marked with a sign, and room to park several vehicles and horse trailers.

Maps Flat Tops NE

From the time you leave the trailhead, you climb. The first mile is the worst of it, in which you ascend just over 600 feet through an open hillside. You cross Skinny Fish Creek about three-quarters of a mile past the trailhead. A wooden bridge allows hikers to stay dry while crossing the rushing, tumbling 30-foot-wide stream. Horse riders will want to direct their mounts through the water. One-quarter mile past the stream crossing, you come to Trail 1812, which is marked only with a post at the junction. Go east here to stay on Trail 1813.

Past the junction, the trail ascends much more gradually past open grassy meadows. You are often in sight of Skinny Fish Creek, which has a few beaver ponds. Along the way are several stream crossings, none of which are obstacles. Rocks and logs in the water let you avoid getting your feet wet. One crossing that is a bit boggy has a small wooden bridge over it.

Trail 1813 splits 2½ miles from the trailhead. The left fork continues on to Skinny Fish Lake, the right goes to McGinnis Lake. Skinny Fish is a half mile farther; McGinnis is about three-quarters of a mile away. Both lakes sit in a large cirque below the Chinese Wall, rising 1,500 feet to the north, east, and south. The scenery is worth the walk.

Each lake has a path leading around the shoreline. Both have suitable campsites around the lakes.

A small unnamed lake is one-half mile north of Skinny Fish Lake, feeding the inlet stream. Only a dim path follows the inlet stream, leading over numerous downed trees in your way. The effort is worth it, though. The outlet of the small lake is a cascade over rocks and windblown timber. On the Chinese Wall, depending on the season, you'll see several falls cascading down the steep rock face.

Skinny Fish Lake was enlarged at some time in the past by an earth-fill dam. About a quarter mile east of the dam is an unmaintained trail that connects to McGinnis Lake, a short distance south. The unmarked trail is about one-half mile west of Skinny Fish Lake from Trail 1812. Both lakes have fish, brookies and cutthroats.

PICKET PIN–LILY POND TRAIL 1811

Picket Pin Trailhead
UTM 13 304989 E, 4434221 N
Lat/Lon 40° 2' 15,18" N, 107° 17' 8.35" W

Lily Pond Trailhead
UTM 13 302749 E, 4437954 N
Lat/Lon 40° 4' 14.50" N, 107° 18' 46.94 W

Description This trail has two heads; one on Forest Road 205, the other begins east of Forest Road 205 on County Road 8. **Picket Pin Trail** follows Picket Pin Creek for 2 miles before angling cross country to enter the east end of Picket Pin Park. This trail traverses dense spruce and fir forests with fewer aspen parks than the Lily Pond Trail. **Lily Pond Trail** climbs 4.5 miles through stands of aspen, open parks, and scattered patches of spruce, fir, and dead spruce. The trail gets its name from the water lilies that bloom in a pond about 3.5 miles up the trail.

Destination Picket Pin Park or Lily Pond Park; Above Lily Pond Park an undesignated trail connects with the Chinese Wall Trail 1803.

Distance 3.5 miles to Trail 1803, 4.4 miles to Lily Pond Trail 1811, 8.5 miles to Lily Pond Trailhead

Elevation 8,758 at Picket Pin Trailhead; 10,703 at its highest point; 8,649 at Lily Pond Trailhead

Directions to Picket Pin Trailhead From Buford drive 17 miles east on County Road 8, go south 3.3 miles on Forest Road 205. The trailhead is on the east side of the road by Picket Pin Creek, a few feet south of the Anderson Reservoir Trailhead. There's room to park 3 or 4 vehicles. **Directions to Lily Pond Trailhead** On County Road 8 about 25 miles east of Buford and a half mile east of Trappers Lake Road.

Maps Flat Tops NE

The trail generally follows the south side of Picket Pin Creek for the first 3 miles. In that distance, you ascend about 1,500 feet as you work your way through timber and small parks. The last mile of the climb leads through stands of tall spruce. At this point, Trail 1811 turns sharply to the left and heads north to Trail 1803. Hike north on Trail 1803 for 4 miles and you will arrive at the trailhead on County Road 8, a quarter mile west of Ripple Creek Pass.

In the park, Trail 1811 turns to the west and begins a gradual drop. You descend through a scattering of timber and smaller meadows. In many of the meadows in this area, you'll find a plant, the false Solomon's seal, often mistaken for skunk cabbage. This leafy member of the lily family grows in wet, open places, crowding out all other plants and flowers. It blooms in late summer, having blossoms that extend above the leafy part by a foot or so. The flower is white or very pale green.

After a mile, the gradient increases as the trail designation changes to Lily Pond Trail in Lily Pond Park. After crossing the small park, the trail continues west across a mile-long flat before descending again. The path meanders some as it drops faster over the last 2 miles, coming out on County Road 8 at Ripple Creek.

This entire area, though you encounter some climbs, is not difficult walking. It's also good elk country.

ANDERSON RESERVOIR TRAIL

UTM 13 0304894 E, 4434234 N
Lat/Lon 40° 2' 15.74" N, 107° 17' 12.40" W

Description A short walk to a reservoir in a beautiful setting. Occasionally winter kills.

Destination Anderson Reservoir

Distance 1.4 miles

Elevation 8,760 at the trailhead; 9,340 at Anderson Reservoir

Directions to trailhead Seventeen miles east of Buford, go south 3.3 miles on Forest Road 205. The trailhead is on the east side of the road by Picket Pin Creek.

Maps Flat Tops NE

The trail begins nearby and about 100 feet south of the Picket Pin Trail at the parking area but crosses the creek before beginning a short climb. The first half mile of the path climbs a short slope, and then bends to the left to traverse a slope for a half mile before swinging northeast. The trail leads through timber the entire distance until you get close to the reservoir, which sits in a small meadow surrounded by trees.

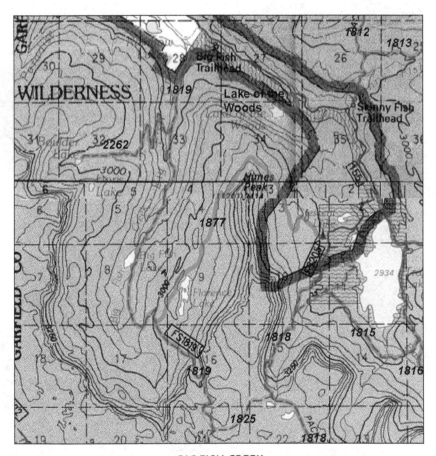

BIG FISH CREEK

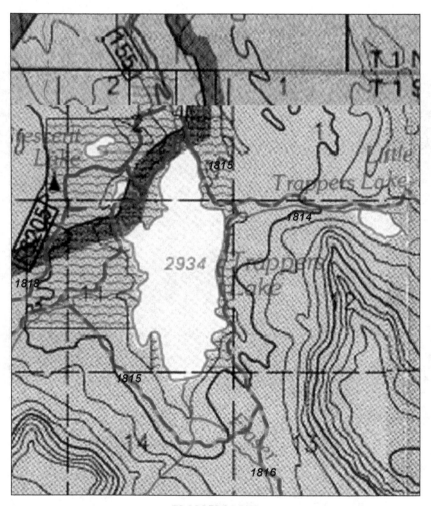

TRAPPERS LAKE

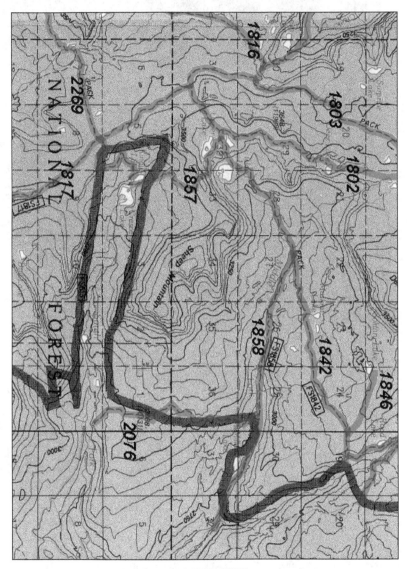

ISLAND LAKES

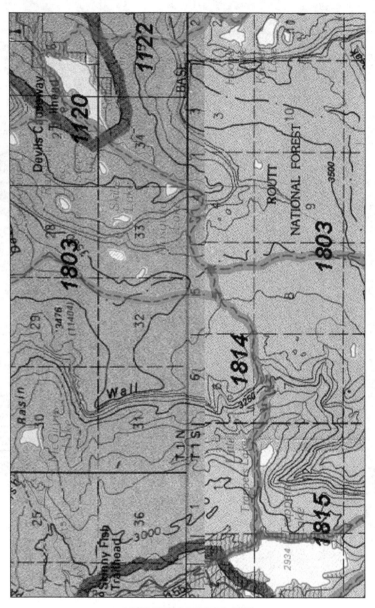

LITTLE TRAPPERS LAKE

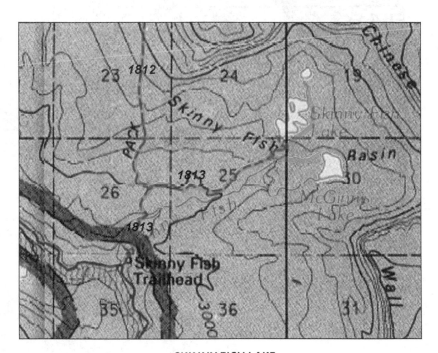

SKINNY FISH LAKE

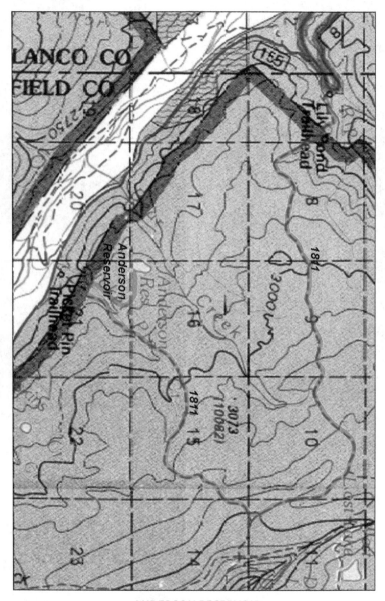

ANDERSON RESERVOIR

7

FOREST ROAD 8 (COUNTY ROAD 8)

Past Forest Road 205 to Trappers Lake, Forest Road 8 continues east past the Ripple Creek Lodge, Ripple Creek Pass Overlook, Trailhead for Trail 1803, and the White River/Routt National Forest boundary.

CHINESE WALL TRAIL 1803

UTM 13 0304338 E, 4441826 N
Lat/Lon 40° 6' 21.21 N, 107° 17' 43.95 W

Description The first mile of the trail follows an abandoned road to the wilderness boundary. It begins as an easy hike with a view of the Lost Lakes Peaks ahead to the south. As the trail nears the peaks, it begins climbing, leading onto the plateau and a view of the entire Flat Tops Wilderness. The route connects with other trails, giving access to the east half of the wilderness. This is a good trail for a horse ride.

Destination Trail 1103, Trail 1812, Devils Causeway, Trail 1814 and Trail 1120, Trail 1802, Trail 1817

Distance 4 miles to Trail 1103, 4.5 miles to Trail 1812, 10.6 miles to Devils Causeway Trail, 12.5 miles to Trails 1814 and 1120, 17.7 miles to Trail 1802, 21 miles to Trail 1817

Elevation 10,276 at the trailhead; 11,730 at Lost Lakes Peaks along the Chinese Wall; 11,347 at Trail 1842

Directions to trailhead On County Road 8 about 25 miles east of Buford and a quarter mile west of Ripple Creek Pass. Park by the corral on the south side of the road or in the large parking area across the road to the north.

Maps Flat Tops NE

You begin your hike on a broad path leading through pine and spruce, and across open meadows. The trail has a few moderate ups and downs. Intermittent streams drain the area, providing a water source in spring and wet years. The streams form boggy areas that will be sloppy early in the season, forcing you to detour around some of the wettest areas.

You get your first peek at the Lost Lakes Peaks as you enter the opening one-half mile from the trailhead. Actually a ridgeline, the plateau slopes steeply to the west, forming the small peaks reaching to nearly 12,000 feet. Looking to the west, you'll see the plateau above the North Fork of the White River. In the distance, the Little Marvine and Big Marvine Peaks rise above the plateau.

The trail continues meandering in a southerly direction, leading through open woods and broad parks. At 2.5 miles, the trail enters a 1.5-mile-long meadow. Abundant moisture produces forage for elk. From the north end of the park, you have a view of the chain of peaks above the Lost Lakes in the basin to the east.

East of Ripple Creek's headwaters begins a moderate ascent, taking you across a lightly wooded slope to the ridge below the peaks. On top of the ridge, you connect with Trail 1103, which leads east into the Lost Lakes basin. If the Lost Lakes are your destination, this trail is the easiest route, though it is a mile longer than taking the Picket Pin Creek Trail from Forest Road 205.

Yes, it's a bit narrow, only a few feet. But the view on each side is great.

From the junction with Trail 1103, Trail 1803 follows the ridge, heading uphill. One-half mile up the way is the junction of Trail 1812, which leads down to Trail 1813, 3 miles away. Trail 1803 begins climbing more steeply from here, following switchbacks up the steep slope.

A mile after the junction with Trail 1812, Trail 1803 emerges into the open. As you hike along the edge of the Lost Lakes Peaks, your view of the wilderness is unimpeded. You look east to Mandall Pass, south to the Devils Causeway, and west to Trappers and Marvine Peaks. To the north, you see Pagoda Peak, its form resembling the temples found in Asia.

The Chinese Wall Trail 1803 continues along the east edge of the rim, giving a view of the Lost Lakes to the east, and south to Causeway Lake. The trail wanders along the plateau for 5 miles to connect with the Devils Causeway Trail. (The Devils Causeway Trail is not recommended to connect with Trail 1119 due to severe erosion of the fractured basalt.) Between Lost Lakes Peaks and Trail 1814, there's no water so carry plenty.

Past the Causeway, Trail 1803 continues south over the high, nearly featureless plateau 3 more miles to connect with Trail 1814. This route will take you 4 miles west down to Trappers Lake.

If you stay on Trail 1803, the path turns east for a half mile to join Trail 1120 (as an alternate hike, you can choose to turn east on Trail 1120 for 4 miles to reach the Stillwater Trailhead). Trail 1803 then heads south again, leading past unnamed potholes as you cross the plateau. Though the trail is high, above 11,000 feet, the walk isn't difficult.

Trail 1803 connects with Trail 1802 2 miles south of the Bear River Trail 1120. The Chinese Wall Trail 1803 continues wandering south. At 2 miles, it begins a descent across a low but steep slope. In this area, Trail 1803 connects with the path leading north 1.25 miles to Surprise Lake. South of the junction with the Surprise Lake trail, Trail 1803 crosses a small flat past a few unnamed lakes. The trail ends at a three-way junction, where it joins Trail 1817. You have several options here so check the map and decide what you prefer to do.

DEER LAKE TRAIL 1802

UTM 13S 311642 E. 4421896 N
Lat/Lon 39° 55′ 38″ N, 107° 12′ 33″ W

Description The trail leaves the plateau and follows a north–south rim above the Middle Fork of Derby Creek. Connects Trails 1803 and 1842.

Destination Deer Lake, Island Lakes

Distance 1.3 miles to Deer Lake, 4 miles to Island Lakes

Elevation 11,590 at Trail 1803; 11,130 at Deer Lake; 11,226 at Trail 1842

Directions to trail On County Road 8 about 25 miles east of Buford and a quarter mile west of Ripple Creek Pass. Park by the corral on the south side of the road or in the large parking area across the road to the north. Accessed from Trail 1803, 3 miles south of Trail 1814, or from Trail 1842 in the Island Lakes area.

Maps Flat Tops NE

Deer Lake Trail 1802 departs Trail 1803 along the plateau among a group of pothole lakes. After walking east 1.3 miles, Trail 1802 heads south, descending across low, steep bluffs on the way to Deer Lake. The lake sits on a small flat overlooking the Middle Fork of Derby Creek to the east.

Past Deer Lake, the trail climbs a low but steep slope, then continues in a southerly direction along a broad ledge, making a gradual descent to the Island Lakes.

(Deer Lake can more easily be accessed from Forest Road 613 at Crescent and Mackinaw Lakes by Trail 1857. By the Island Lakes, Trail 1802 connects with Trail 1842. Go left a quarter mile, or right a half mile to junctions with Trail 1802, then head north to Deer Lake.)

8

FOREST ROAD 16

Ripple Creek Pass is the boundary of the White River and Routt National Forests. On the east side of this divide, the road designation changes from Forest Road 8 to Forest Road 16. Some maps also show it designated as Rio Blanco County Road 8 until it reaches the Routt County line.

A campground is located at Vaughn Lake on the south beside the road, 4 miles east of Ripple Creek Pass. Another 3 miles east beyond the campground is Forest Road 962, which heads to the south. A sign here reads "Trail 1172 Transfer." Forest Road 962 ends a mile to the south at a gate near the wilderness boundary.

The Pyramid Guard Station is on Forest Road 16 , 2 miles past the junction with Forest Road 962. One mile beyond the Pyramid Guard Station is the trailhead for Trail 1200, leading to Pyramid Peak. Another 2.5 miles takes you to the junction of Forest Road 16 and Rio Blanco County Road 55. Go right (east) to stay on Forest Road 16. About 10 miles farther east on Forest Road 16, after crossing Dunkley Pass, is the junction with Forest Road 959. Forest Road 959 goes south to Sheriff Reservoir and gives access to Trail 1117.

The Routt County line is 6 more miles to the east beyond the junction with Forest Road 959. At this point, Forest Road 16 becomes Routt County Road 132. Four miles past the county line, the road divides. The branch to the left is Routt County Road 15 and takes you to Phippsburg. The right is Routt County Road 17 and goes into Yampa. At both towns, the roads connect with State Highway 131.

TRANSFER TRAIL 1172

UTM 13 309674E, 4445688N
Lat/Lon 40° 8′ 30.67N, 107° 14′ 2.83W

Description This trail saves a mile of walking when taking Trail 1119 south. It follows a former road and is an easy walk.

Destination Transfer Trailhead on Trail 1119, Blue Mountain Creek

Distance 0.7 mile to Trail 1119, 1.4 miles to Blue Mountain Creek

Elevation 9,020 at gate; 9,270 at junction to Blue Mountain Creek; 9,066 at Trail 1119

Directions to trailhead Four miles east of Ripple Creek Pass on County Road 8 (Forest Road 16) to sign, "Trail 1172 Transfer" at Forest Road 967. South on Forest Road 967, a very rough road 0.7 mile to gate.

Maps Flat Tops NE

Transfer Trail 1172 is an alternate access point to the wilderness. Don't drive your old Pinto down this road to the trailhead unless you don't mind leaving mufflers, bumpers, or other parts along the way. In addition to being rough, it also gets very muddy when it rains.

Past the gate at the trailhead, Transfer Trail 1172 is a former road. It's an easy walk through open forest and small meadows. You'll probably see deer along this trail, too. A 1-mile walk takes you to a fork, the east path leading down to Trail 1119, which is another half mile south. The right fork leads to Blue Mountain Creek and follows it upstream to the west. This meandering meadow stream has small cutthroat in it.

EAST FORK TRAIL 1119

(Pyramid Guard Station Trailhead)
UTM 13 310717E, 4446961 N
Lat/Lon 40° 9' 13.27"N, 107° 13' 19.92" W

Description This trail provides hikers and horseback riders access to the northeast part of the wilderness. You'll follow the East Fork of the Williams Fork, a small stream that eventually joins the Yampa River. The trail gives access to area lakes and takes you near the Devils Causeway, a unique glacially formed structure.

Destination Trail 1172, Trail 1116, Trail 1117, Round Lake and Trail 1116, Causeway Lake, Trail 1120, Stillwater Reservoir Trailhead

Distance 2 miles to Trail 1172, 4 miles to Trail 1116, 6 miles to Trail 1117, 8 miles to Round Lake and Trail 1116, 10 miles to Causeway Lake, 12 miles to Trail 1120, 14 miles to Stillwater Reservoir Trailhead

Elevation 8,415 at Pyramid Guard Station; 11,590 at pass below Devils Causeway; 10,255 at Stillwater Reservoir

Directions to trailhead Six miles east of Ripple Creek Pass on Rio Blanco County Road 8 (Forest Road 16) to Pyramid Guard Station. Or from State Highway 131, go east on Routt County Road 17 for 5.3 miles to County Road 132. Drive west 3.8 miles on County Road 132 and turn west onto Rio Blanco County Road 8. Follow Rio Blanco County Road 23 miles to Pyramid Guard Station. From Yampa, it's nearly 30 miles to the trailhead. Parking is available on the south side of the road across from the Guard Station. Rest facilities available.

Maps Flat Tops NE

The Pyramid Guard Station is neatly hidden in the aspens south of County Road 8. The trail begins here and follows the East Williams Fork, a small creek about 15 feet in width. Legend has it the stream is named for Old Bill Williams, a scout and trapper who explored Colorado's mountains in the 1830s. The trail stays low, near the stream for the first couple of miles. Baldy Creek joins the Williams Fork from the east where you cross the wilderness boundary. Here, the trail begins a gentle but steady ascent through the aspen and spruce forest. A mile farther, the trail crosses shallow Blue Mountain Creek. Watch for deer and elk in this area.

After crossing Blue Mountain Creek, the trail climbs a bit as it goes around the nose of the ridge, then angles upward across the east-facing timbered slope. Continuing south another half mile, Trail 1172 connects from the west. The two paths join at an opening in the timber. Trail 1119 follows the contour across the slope, changing little in elevation over the next 2 miles to the junction of Trail 1116.

Past the junction, Trail 1119 follows switchbacks down to the East Fork of the Williams Fork where it is necessary to ford the stream. The Forest Service advises that this crossing can be dangerous during high water flows. Above you, to the east, the hillside is an aspen forest. As is expected, the colors in the fall are—well—colorful. Late September and early October find the region painted in bright yellows, oranges, and deep crimsons in a magnificent luminescence. The next 2 miles take you through aspen forests and open parks that extend high up the west-facing, steep slopes of 11,532-foot Pyramid

Peak. For the next 2 miles, you follow the Williams Fork upstream along the bottom of the deep valley below the peak. Along this part of the trail, you have a view to the east of the high wall west of Mandall Pass.

The trail ascends the slope east of the stream, where it joins Trail 1117. For the next mile, the Trail 1119 follows along the stream, taking you south. You cross Williams Fork for the last time, and then begin climbing the east-facing slope.

A mile farther south up the trail, you come to Round Lake. It's a beautiful lake, having steep banks on the north side and cutthroats in the water. Just past the lake, you connect with the south end of Trail 1116. A sign marks the junction. A level campsite is located on the northeast side of the lake.

Sometime around 1900, a forest fire burned much of the valley near Round Lake. Foresters say the land has still not entirely recovered from the lightning-caused fire because of the intense heat that robbed most of the soil's nutrients.

Causeway Lake is 1.5 miles past Round Lake, lying in a large open meadow below a nearly vertical—several miles long—wall. This section of the trail is an easy walk, having about as much up as down and nothing severe. Looking to the east reveals the steep wall west of Mandall Pass. The largest draw is Dead Mexican Gulch. It acquired its name as a result of an altercation that occurred here many years ago. See the Mandall Lakes Trail 1121 description for the story.

The trail crosses the outlet of Causeway Lake on logs lying across the small stream. A small pool has formed here below the lake's dam and during spawning runs is crowded with cutthroat trout. You'll be able to see them easily in the clear water as they move around searching for tasty tidbits floating down to them. Some fish approach 16 inches in length.

The dam of the lake appears to have been built by beavers. Actually, it's hard to tell if the lake is a large beaver pond or has just been enlarged by the furry engineers. The lake is shallow and has a grassy shoreline that is quite sloppy to walk through, making it interesting to get close enough to fish.

Good campsites can be found on the northwest side of the lake, well away from the shoreline. A short distance from the beaver ponds at the west inlet to Causeway Lake, several springs are tucked away in the hummocks that have slumped on the unstable slope. One spring is 4 feet wide where the water pours down a rocky slope. The water is good and probably safe to drink without treatment. And it's cold. Refreshing. Almost as good as a beer.

Along the east side of Causeway Lake, Trail 1119 leads through the timbered shoreline, then begins a more rapid, though not steep ascent through smaller stands of timber and meadows. Watch for deer and elk in this area. There are several openings where cow elk and their calves like to graze.

A mile above Causeway Lake, you pass a tiny creek, the last place to get water until you're on the south side of Devils Causeway, a distance of about 3 miles. Since the ascent is dehydrating, you may want to fill your canteens here. Be sure to treat the water. Past the creek, the trail climbs steeply to Devils Causeway. The last mile is rocky and a bit loose underfoot. Once on the pass, pause to view the scenery. Back to the north, you'll see Causeway Lake and in the distance, you can see a piece of Round Lake, partially hidden in the dense spruce timber.

Across the valley to the south and several miles in the distance is the broad flat slope of Flat Top Mountain, the highest point in the wilderness.

Above you to the west lies the tip of Devils Causeway, having a path to the top of the narrow ridge. (Crossing the Devils Causeway is not recommended due to severe erosion of the basalt rock.) For a description, see the listing under State Highway 131.

At the pass, you can go east on the west part of Trail 1121 (not shown on most maps) up the alpine meadow slope, then head north to Mandall Pass.

Trail 1119 descends the steep walls of a cirque. Switchbacks make the grade easier, but in places the dirt is loose and the footing tricky. Stay on the trail here, as the soils are fragile and easily eroded. After crossing a talus slope, you pass Little Causeway Lake to the west of the trail and a mile below Devils Causeway. Once past the lake, the trail becomes flatter and easier to walk. Near the wilderness boundary, you pass a shallow, grungy-looking pond before connecting with Trail 1120. Past this junction, it's 1 more mile to the Stillwater Trailhead along the shore of Stillwater Reservoir.

LOST LAKES TRAIL 1116

UTM 13 311907 E, 4441706 N
Lat/Lon 40° 6′ 23.54″ N, 107° 12′ 24.52″ W

Description The trail gives access to the Lost Lakes area from Trail 1119. Fishing is excellent for brook and cutthroat trout.

Destination Trail 1103, Lost Lakes, Long Lake, Round Lake

Distance 3 miles to Trail 1103, 4 miles to Lost Lakes, 5 miles to Long Lake, 6 miles to Round Lake

Elevation 9,285 at north junction; 10,720 between East Lost Lake and Long Lake; 10,420 at Round Lake

**Lost Lakes Peak is visible from the Ripple Creek Overlook,
a short distance west of Ripple Creek Pass.**

Directions to trail On Forest Road 16 4 miles south from Pyramid Guard Station on Trail 1119, or 7 miles north on Trail 1119 from Stillwater Reservoir.

Maps Flat Tops NE

On the nose of a small ridge above a stream named the West Fork, Lost Lakes Trail 1116 heads uphill to the west from Trail 1119. Trail 1116 follows the ridge up through the timber, coming into a meadow after a half-mile hike. In the clearing, the grade becomes less but still climbs, following the small creek. At the south end of the meadow, the trail wanders away from the stream, following a low ridge above two forks of the West Fork.

After 3 miles, the trail crosses a low divide and enters a large meadow. Here, you have a view of the Lost Lakes Peaks and the vertical wall that trends southeast above the basin. Immediately below the divide, ahead in the meadow, sits a small, shallow lake known as the Retaining Pond. It's fed by springs saturating the willow-covered slopes on the west. South of the pond, the trail connects with Trail 1103, which heads west toward the Lost Lakes Peaks.

Trail 1116 goes south across the small meadow. You encounter a couple of stream crossings. The water is deep. Be careful early in the season when you need to move off the trail to find a way over the water. Past the meadow, the trail takes you through the timber. The climb isn't tough but you'll encounter log steps placed across the trail to reduce erosion. Once you get past the steps, about .01 of a mile, you reach East Lost Lake. Its water is clear and deep. The view west is impressive; the glacially carved wall of rock imposes on the basin, diverting attention from everything else.

Continuing on past East Lost, Trail 1116 wanders along the steep north bank of the lake, then begins a gentle climb that ends a mile farther, where you cross a low, broad divide. On the downhill side, another mile of hiking takes you to Long Lake. The lake is oriented east–west. It's long and narrow and you'll become frustrated at seeing large cutthroats that swim past, ignoring your offerings.

At the west end of the lake, you can walk south a few yards over glacial rubble to three other, smaller lakes. Past Long Lake, it's an easy half-mile walk on Trail 1116 to Round Lake.

If you feel ambitious, try getting off the trails in this area. You'll have to pick your way over, around, and sometimes under the randomly stacked downed timber. If you're quiet, though, and observant, you'll have a good chance of seeing elk. If nothing else, you'll at least see an abundance of fresh sign from their passing.

The ground in the area of these lakes is hummocky, rough, and uneven. The walk isn't difficult but really pleasant campsites are not overly abundant because of this. You'll be able to find sites for a small backpack tent but expect to look around to find something reasonably level, especially on weekends.

The Lost Lakes area was the scene of a second fire to occur in the summer of 2002. It also was caused by lightning.

WEST LOST LAKE TRAIL 1103

UTM 13 310312 E, 4438461 N
Lat/Lon 40° 4' 37.20" N, 107° 13' 27.94" W

Description This short trail gives access to lakes below the Lost Lakes Peaks.

Destination Deep Lake, West Lost Lake, Trail 1803

Distance 0.5 mile to Deep Lake , 1 mile to West Lost Lake, 2 miles to Trail 1803

Elevation 10,080 at Trail 1116; 10,660 at Trail 1803

Directions to trail Begin at Trail 1803 0.4 mile west of Ripple Creek Pass. Hike southeast 3.5 miles to Trail 1103. Accessed from Trail 1116, 3 miles from the junction of Trails 1119 and 1116 along the East Fork of Williams Fork.

Maps Flat Tops NE

Trail 1103 leaves Trail 1116 in a large meadow just south of the Retaining Pond. Trail 1103 heads west in the open before entering the trees and beginning an easy ascent. The trail makes a bend to the right at a creek crossing one-half mile from the junction. On the left, you'll see a path leading up a short hill. It's not marked and is not maintained, but it leads to Deep Lake, a quarter mile south.

After stepping across the tiny creek, the main trail resumes its easy climb. Along the way, you pass a small meadow. During the spring and early summer, the area can be extremely wet. It's another half mile to West Lost Lake, surrounded by dense timber. Campsites are limited. To enjoy a quality wilderness experience and preserve the area for others, avoid the overused area beside the trail. Finding other sites in the trees is difficult because of the uneven ground and downed trees. A better choice for camping may be the meadow north of the lake and on the head of the West Fork creek. It's flat and near water. The timber in this area burned in the 2002 fire.

At the lake, the trail climbs onto the ridge north of Lost Lakes Peaks. The ascent is somewhat steep in places but not bad. Once on the divide, you have a view of the basin to the east and the plateau in the distance.

BLACK MOUNTAIN TRAIL 1117

UTM 13 317844 E, 4446202 N
Lat/Lon 40° 8' 53.71" N, 107° 7' 24.94"

Description From Sheriff Reservoir, the trail follows the wilderness boundary to the Pyramid Peak area, and then meanders through meadows and open woodlands to join Trail 1119. The area along the trail is quite primitive, used primarily during hunting seasons.

Destination Trail 1200, Trail 1119

Distance 3 miles to Trail 1200, 5.5 miles to Trail 1119

Elevation 9,780 at Sheriff Reservoir; 11,100 east of Trail 1200; 9,730 at Trail 1119

Directions to trailhead From County Road 8 (Forest Road 16), 4 miles east of Dunkley Pass or 11 miles west of Yampa, go south on Forest Road 959 4 miles to west side of Sheriff Reservoir and end of road.

Maps Flat Tops NE

Trail 1117 heads southwest from Sheriff Reservoir, taking you to the wilderness boundary, 0.5 mile away. The trail follows an old logging road for the first mile through a large meadow for 2.5 miles before entering the wilderness. Along the way, you climb rather quickly and are soon nearly 1,000 feet above the reservoir, which you'll see to the east. The trail turns south, still ascending, though less abruptly now. The grade begins to flatten, then starts a gentle descent through the timber. You break into a small clearing that soon opens into a large meadow south of the trail. The high point on the trail gives a view of Pyramid Peak, a mile west. Looking north, you'll see Dunkley Pass and the Dunkley Flat Tops. Sand Point, at 11,182 feet, is also visible to the east. At 3 miles from the trailhead, you connect with Trail 1200.

From here, Trail 1117 continues its easy descent, leading through small stands of trees and across open parks, giving you the opportunity to see deer and elk. Those with sharp eyes will often be rewarded. The meadow soon becomes transformed into a low stream valley as you continue downward. The path becomes steeper as you cross Black Mountain Creek, and then works its way around a spruce-fir covered ridge. You come into a large, steep hillside clearing as you follow across the slope downhill to connect with Trail 1119.

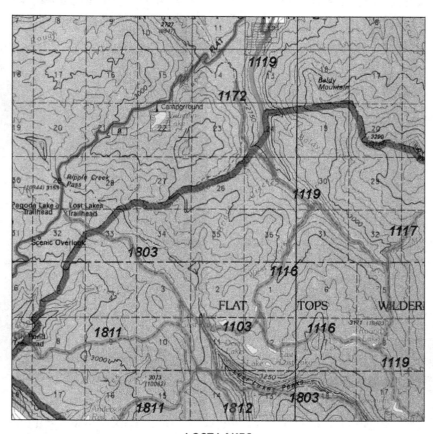

LOST LAKES

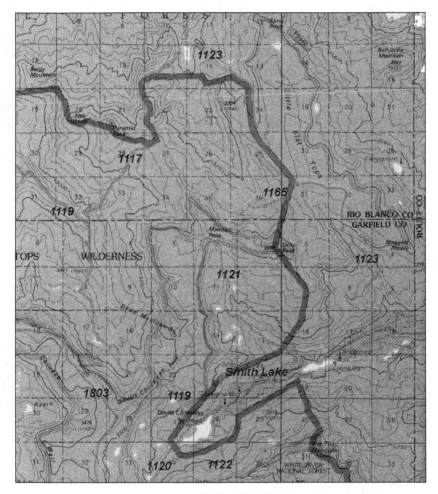

MANDALL LAKES

9

STATE HIGHWAY 131

Several trails on the east and northeast side of the Flat Tops are accessed from State Highway 131. The good paved highway runs north from the community of Wolcott on Interstate 70 to Steamboat Springs. Along the way, the road passes several small ranching and mining communities.

From Interstate 70, exit at Wolcott and head north 15 miles on State Highway 131 to State Bridge on the Colorado River. Two more miles to Bond, another wide place in the road. The next town is McCoy, 4 miles farther north. Less than a mile north from McCoy, Eagle County Road 301 heads southwest at the county line, which follows the Colorado River to Interstate 70. Twelve miles west on County Road 301 you come to Burns and another mile takes you to Derby Junction. Both places connect with Derby Mesa Loop, a rough road that gives access to Forest Road 613, an even rougher four-wheel-drive road that ends at Crescent and Mackinaw Lakes. From here Trail 1857 climbs a bluff leading to the three Island Lakes inside the wilderness.

Southwest past Derby Junction the Sweetwater Road leads northwest past Sweetwater Lake to the Turret Creek Trailhead. Some of the steepest trails originate here.

Southwest on County Road 301 you come to Deep Creek at Forest Road 600, which gives access to the south side of the wilderness. Two miles farther south takes you to Dotsero and Interstate 70.

Continuing north from McCoy on State Highway 131, you reach the junction of State Highway 134, the Gore Pass Highway, and the store/gas station at Toponas.

Nine miles north of Toponas is the town of Yampa. Turn west on Moffat Avenue at the convenience store/service station and go

Pyramid Peak is a prominent landmark on the east side of the Flat Tops Wilderness Area, seen here from State Highway 131.

one-third mile to Routt County Road 7, the road to Stillwater Reservoir and trailheads to the wilderness. National forest and wilderness information is available at the Yampa Ranger Station, 300 Roselawn Ave. At the north end of Yampa, less than a half mile farther along State Highway 131, you can turn west on County Road 17. Drive 5.5 miles west on County Road 17 to the junction with County Road 132. Turn west onto County Road 132, which becomes Rio Blanco County Road 8 at the Routt/Rio Blanco county line, and drive west along the north side of the Flat Tops.

Going 6 miles north on State Highway 131 out of Yampa takes you to Phippsburg. It's 4 more miles to Oak Creek, another jumping-off place for the Flat Tops. Head west on Routt County Road 25, which joins County Road 132. Go west on County Road 132 to connect with Rio Blanco County Road 8.

From Oak Creek, Steamboat Springs is another 22 miles north along State Highway 131.

Routt County Road 7

At Moffat Avenue exit State Highway 131 by the convenience store/ service station. Follow Moffat Avenue west through Yampa. The street ends at the stop sign in front of a general store. To the south, you'll see a sign indicating that Stillwater Reservoir lies to the west along Routt County Road 7. It's about 17 miles to the reservoir.

Inside the Routt National Forest, County Road 7 is designated Forest Road 900. This road gives access to Coal Creek, Mandall Lakes, Smith Lake, Mosquito Lake, and Hooper and Keener Lakes Trails.

SAND CREEK TRAIL 1123

UTM 13 325576 E, 4436014 N
Lat/Lon 40° 3′ 29.76″ N, 107° 2′ 41.85° W
Coordinates are at Forest Road 900 and Forest Road 906

Description The trail begins one-half mile from Forest Road 900 by following County Road 157 to the trailhead. It then follows the boundary, taking you across the Little Flat Tops to Sheriff Reservoir. This is a good place to get away as it is seldom used. A forest ranger said there are lots of elk in the area.

Destination Trail 1165, Sheriff Reservoir

Distance 4 miles to Trail 1165, 7 miles to Sheriff Reservoir

Elevation 10,140 at trailhead; 9,920 at outlet of Sheriff Reservoir

Directions to trailhead From Yampa go 11.9 miles west on County Road 7 and Forest Road 900 to Forest Road 906 (County Road 157), a rough road requiring a high-clearance vehicle. Sign on Forest Road 900 reads "Sawtooth Portal." You will need a four-wheel-drive vehicle when the road is muddy. The trailhead is one-half mile from the junction. Park off the road by the gate.

Maps Flat Tops NE

The Little Flat Tops is an extension of the Flat Tops Plateau. It's sort of a miniature of the main feature of the wilderness. The Little Flat Tops is just outside the wilderness but it's still a roadless area.

Sandcreek Trail 1123 is a road, now closed, that follows the East Coal Creek. The route forks one-half mile from the trailhead. The right fork dead ends to the north in another one-half mile, below a peak named Maggies Nipple. Sort of makes you wonder who Maggie was and the story behind the name of the peak.

The left fork of the trail crosses East Coal Creek, and then continues north along the bottom of the valley up a gradual ascent. The valley is flat and marshy at the lower end but the trail stays above the soft goo. The grade is gentle as you continue north upstream along Coal Creek, named for coal found along its banks. The valley is timbered on the west side but your view up the east side is unimpeded. The bottom flattens out a second time, another boggy area. This time, the trail leads almost through the wetland for a short distance. At the upper end of the bog, you enter a broad meadow at the bottom of gentle slopes on either side. Continue up Coal Creek to near its head before ascending the slope leading onto the Little Flat Tops. As you climb higher up the valley, past the bogs, you have a view of Orno Peak to the west. It's one of the higher peaks on the Flat Tops.

Here, the plateau is broad, having little relief. Directly north lie a few unnamed lakes that feed into Coal Creek. You have a view of Orno Peak to the south and a bit west, rising to 12,133 feet. The peak sits at the end of a long, narrow ridge unencumbered by trees. The summit and its steep south-trending slope mark the boundary of the wilderness. Trail 1123 leads west across the flat for nearly a mile, taking you to the wilderness boundary.

At the edge of the wilderness, the trail connects with Trail 1165, which heads west to an unnamed lake. Trail 1123 turns north and begins a barely noticeable descent leading into the Sand Creek drainage. The trail follows the small trickle of water as it travels through the low, broad gully. Continuing north 2 miles from the trail junction, Sand Creek has eroded the drainage, making it deeper, its sides steeper. The trail crosses Sand Creek and meanders through a willow thicket, now leading down across the steepening slope on the east. Another 2 miles takes you to a group of small lakes having names like Crater, Sand, Camel, and Spring. The ground around them is hummocky. You travel northwest another mile, now descending the nose of a broad low ridge where you enter the open at the north end of Sheriff Reservoir and Forest Road 969. The reservoir is at the trailheads of Trails 1117 and 1123.

SAWTOOTH TRAIL 1165

UTM 13 322117 E, 4441054 N
Lat/Lon 40° 6' 10.65" N, 107° 5' 13.08" W

Description This is a good place to get away as the area is seldom used. A forest ranger said there are lots of elk in the area. Once inside the wilderness, the terrain is hummocky as you enter a broad drainage north of 12,133-foot Orno Peak. The trail ends near an unnamed lake in the headwaters of Trout Creek. In the past the lake was reported to have cutthroat trout. During the depression of the '30s, local miners panned gold from the stream. The flat ground and scattered timber provide campsites if you plan to stay overnight here.

Destination: Unnamed lake inside the wilderness UTM 13T 319533E, 4440303N; Lat/Lon 40° 05' 44"N, 107° 07' 01"W

Distance 1.5 miles

Elevation 11,040 at junction with Trail 1165; 10,960 at end of trail

Directions to trail At Yampa drive 11.7 miles west on County Road 7 (this road changes into Forest Road 900 inside the Routt National Forest) to County Road 157. Go north on County Road 157 1 mile to the Sand Creek trailhead. The road is gated at trailhead. From the Sand Creek Trailhead on Forest Road 900, hike 3 miles north on Trail 1123 to the junction with Trail 1165. Head west on Trail 1165 2 miles to the lake.

Maps Flat Tops NE

MANDALL LAKES TRAIL 1121

UTM 13 322834 E, 4434774 N
Lat/Lon 40° 2' 47.12" N, 107° 4' 36.31" W

Description This route takes you past the Mandall Lakes, all but one good for fishing. Directly north of Black Mandall Lake, you climb to nearly 12,000 feet on Mandall Pass, then head south over high, rolling tundra. Campsites can be found near the Mandall Lakes. Mandall Pass is 1.5 miles past Black Mandall Lake. From Mandall Pass, Trail 1121 heads south above timberline and connects with Trail 1119 below the Devils Causeway.

Destination Mandall Lakes, Mandall Pass

Distance 4 miles to Mandall Lakes, 5 miles to Mandall Pass

Elevation 9,765 at Mandall Trailhead; 11,980 at Mandall Pass

Directions to trailhead From Yampa, drive 13.9 miles west on County Road 7 (this road changes into Forest Road 900 inside the Routt National Forest) to the trailhead. The trailhead is well marked with a sign. Parking is on the south side of the road beside Yampa Reservoir.

Map Flat Tops NE

On the way to the trailhead, you drive by Yamcola Reservoir. During the construction of the dam, a leg bone of a mastodon was uncovered here.

After climbing the first slope, the trail parallels Mandall Creek. You'll wander in and out of the timber and walk through sloping open hillsides as you make your way to the Mandall Lakes. Aspens on the lower slopes make this a colorful walk in the fall. After crossing Mandall Creek, you hike through Engelmann spruce and subalpine fir forest. Where the trail follows the stream bottom, the climb is noticeable. The woodlands are broken at times along the way by long, narrow meadows.

Hikers are asked to register at trailheads. It doesn't include the dogs, but the Forest Service requests that they be kept on leash or under control.

After following the drainage 2.5 miles, you arrive at a small shelf that holds four of the five lakes; Mud Mandall Lake, the two Twin Mandall Lakes, and Slide Mandall Lake. Black Mandall Lake is 0.5 mile farther north. Campsites can be found near each of the lakes. From the small clearings at the lakes, you can see 12,133-foot Orno Peak, 2 miles to the northeast.

After passing the five Mandall Lakes, you pass several near the trail that are unnamed. Beyond these, you enter an alpine meadow as you climb toward Mandall Pass, a mile farther north. The trail climbs rather steeply at the head of the broad glacially carved valley. Just south of the pass, you reach almost 12,000 feet without even ascending a peak. Even in late summer, you'll often encounter snow here.

The USFS map shows it as Trail 1121, and not marked on NGS Trappers Lake map. Here you can head south over the tundra-like plateau. You have spectacular views along the way, making the walk worth the effort. The trail is about 5 miles to connect with the east end of Devils Causeway. Be aware that you may encounter unfavorable

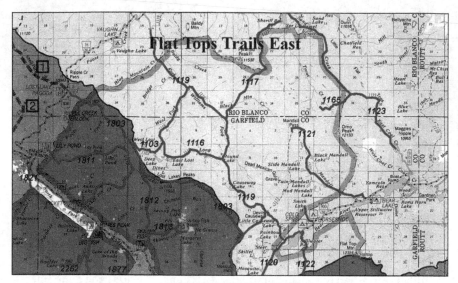

FLAT TOPS TRAILS EAST

weather conditions in a place offering no shelter from the elements. Expect high winds, cool air, bright sun, and changing conditions. Go prepared. Carry water as none is available.

About 2 miles south of Mandall Pass on Trail 1121, along the most narrow section on the flat, you overlook Dead Mexican Gulch, descending to the west. Eric Petterson, a Wilderness Ranger on the Yampa District, told me how the place acquired its name.

Petterson said one account of the story is recorded in letters to the wife of the Ranger who patrolled the area long before the region was designated as a wilderness. The story varies, depending on the source. In one version, two sheepherders quarreled, the disagreement ending with one murdering the other. The body of the dead sheepherder, who had murdered two people north of Steamboat Springs, fell into a campfire and was burned. His remains were buried in the gulch in 1921. Another version has the Mexican's death occurring as the result of an accident. The grave site is marked on topo and Forest Service maps but Petterson said it is difficult to locate.

Hike past Mandall Pass for 4 miles on Trail 1121 over the open land to Devils Causeway. Carry plenty of water as none is available after leaving the Mandall Lakes until you reach Little Causeway Lake, a distance of nearly 7 miles.

Going north at Devils Causeway, you can descend to Causeway Lake and continue on to Pyramid Guard Station. By following Trail 1119 south, you can return to your starting point by way of Stillwater Trailhead and Forest Road 900 to the Mandall Lakes Trailhead.

SMITH LAKE TRAIL

UTM 13 319603 E, 4433276 N
Lat/Lon 40° 1' 55.72" N, 107° 5' 50.92" W

Description A short, easy hike

Destination Smith Lake

Distance 0.8 mile

Elevation 10,192 at trailhead; 10,507 at Smith Lake

Directions to trailhead From Yampa, drive 16.7 miles west on County Road 7 (this road changes into Forest Road 900 inside the Routt National Forest) 0.2 mile past Horseshoe Campground. The trailhead is marked. Park along the road.

Maps Flat Tops NE

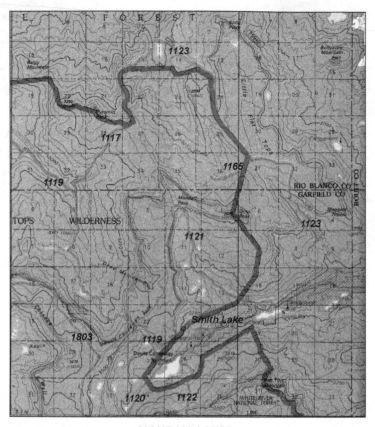

MANDALL LAKES

The trail crosses Cold Springs Creek, and then enters a lightly timbered spruce and fir forest as it heads north to Smith Lake. The hike is short and the trail an easy climb. The wilderness boundary lies along the south shoreline. The shallow lake, surrounded by trees, reportedly holds cutthroat trout, some of good size. Lower Smith Lake is about 200 yards south of Smith Lake. It is reported to have small cutts. Camping is prohibited within a quarter mile of the lake.

The lake and creek are named for Tom Smith, a trapper who lived in the surrounding mountains about 1880. One story told of him says he crawled into the den of a grizzly bear, shot it, and sold the fat for ten cents a pound.

Cold Springs Creek earned its name because of its very cold water. Even in summer, the temperature of the creek averages 35°F.

EAST FORK TRAIL 1119
(STILLWATER RESERVOIR TRAILHEAD)

UTM 13 318859 E, 4432761 N
Lat/Lon 40° 1' 38.95" N, 107° 7' 21.94" W

Description The trail gives access to area lakes and takes you onto the Devils Causeway, a unique glacially formed structure. You'll follow the East Fork of the Williams Fork, a small stream that eventually joins the Yampa River.

Destination Trail 1120, Devils Causeway, Causeway Lake, Trail 1116 and Round Lake, Trail 1117, Trail 1116, Trail 1172

Distance 1 mile to Trail 1120, 3 miles to Devils Causeway, 5.5 miles to Causeway Lake, 7 miles to Round Lake, 9 miles to Trail 1117, 11.5 miles to Trail 1116, 14 miles to Transfer Trailhead

Elevation 10,360 at Stillwater Reservoir; 11,590 at pass below Devils Causeway; 8,415 at Pyramid Guard Station

Directions to trailhead From Yampa, go 17 miles west on Routt County Road 7 (this road changes into Forest Road 900 inside the Routt National Forest) to Stillwater Reservoir.

Maps Flat Tops NE

DEVILS CAUSEWAY

UTM 13T 316552 E, 4433790 N
Lat/Lon 40° 01′ 23″ N, 107° 09′ 40″ W

Description The Devils Causeway is a unique geologic structure in the Flat Tops Wilderness. The area was created by fire and ice. Lava covered the region to a great thickness, which was later carved into valleys by glaciers. At the Causeway, the glacier nearly succeeded in wearing away the basalt, leaving only a tall, thin wall, rising vertically more than 1,000 feet above two drainages. At one point, the wall is narrow— very narrow—less than 4 feet in width. At that point, the Causeway is a jumble of broken rock. Footing is tricky getting across the knifelike ridge. And while the view is spectacular and the feeling one can enjoy while standing above two rugged vistas is exhilarating, it's not a place for those having a fear of heights. The actual danger, though, is more perceived than real.

Destination Devils Causeway

Distance 3 miles

Elevation 11749

Directions to trailhead From Yampa, drive 17.4 miles west on County Road 7 (this road changes into Forest Road 900 inside the Routt National Forest) to Stillwater Reservoir. Parking is available at the marked trailhead at the end of the road. Hike 0.7 mile west on Trail 1119, then north 2.3 miles to the Causeway.

Maps Flat Tops NE

For some reason a few people do this on hands and knees. It's only 500 feet to the bottom on each side. I had to hang on to Skipper since he wasn't concerned about the height.

Take Trail 1119 0.7 mile along the north shoreline of the reservoir. Go north at the junction with Trail 1120, ascending to the Causeway, 3 miles from the trailhead. A well-used path leads up the steep slope to the west, taking you to one of the more magnificent vistas in the wilderness. From the ridge, you have unobstructed views in all directions. You'll see several of the many peaks, including Flat Top Mountain to the south, the highest point in the wilderness. To the northwest, you can observe the highest point along the ridge, the Lost Lakes Peaks. Look southwest into the Bear River valley to see a series of lakes below the Causeway, tucked away among the trees. Above them, the ridge broadens to a width of 3 or 4 miles. To the west, Big Marvine Peak rises from the plateau, as do the three smaller Little Marvine Peaks some distance north. In addition to the peaks and high plateau, the many lakes seen from this vantage point will fascinate you.

The Causeway is a popular day hike, perhaps too popular. The last half mile, which is above timberline, leads through fragile, easily eroded terrain. Careless hikers have damaged portions of the slope by shortcutting switchbacks. Because of the short growing season at this altitude (above 11,000 feet), restoration of native vegetation is a slow process. Unless hikers stay on the maintained trail, rangers may be forced to close the area to prevent further damage.

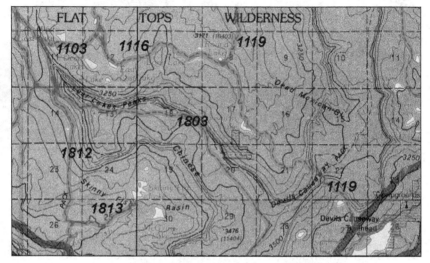

DEVILS CAUSEWAY

BEAR RIVER TRAIL 1120

UTM 13 317907 E, 4432320 N
Lat/Lon 40° 1′ 24.31″ N, 107° 8′ 1.63″ W

Description The hike begins at the East Fork Trailhead, Trail 1119 at Stillwater Reservoir. Trail 1120 begins 0.7 mile from the trailhead. This trail wanders through spruce forest past Mosquito Lake before climbing the headwall onto the plateau. At the junction of Trail 1803, on the plateau, is the White River National Forest boundary. You can continue west to connect with Trail 1814 and descend to Trappers Lake.

Destination Trail 1120, Mosquito Lake, Trail 1803

Distance 0.7 mile to Trail 1120, 2.5 miles to Mosquito Lake, 4 miles to Trail 1803

Elevation 10,280 at trailhead; 11,412 at Trail 1803

Directions to trailhead From Yampa, drive 17 miles west on County Road 7 (this road changes into Forest Road 900 inside the Routt National Forest) to Stillwater Reservoir. Parking is available at the end of the road. Follow Trail 1119 1 mile west to the junction of Trail 1120.

Maps Flat Tops NE

The first mile of the trail takes you along the north shoreline of Stillwater Reservoir. The lake was constructed during the 1930s to supply irrigation water to the area ranches. It gets its name from the narrow gorge that once held the flow of several streams forming an area of still water.

You connect with Trail 1120 after 0.7 mile. Heading west along Trail 1120, you enter spruce and fir forest as you follow the Bear River upstream. The river was given its name by early fur trappers. You pass Mosquito Lake 1.5 miles west past the junction, which shares a large flat with three other lakes; Skillet Lake, Steer Lake, and Rainbow Lake. No designated trails lead to the lakes but you will be able to hike cross-country to each.

Past Mosquito Lake, the trail continues generally to the southwest, following Bear River upstream another half mile, then bears right to ascend the glacially carved wall that extends south from Devils Causeway. Switchbacks make the climb easier. Once you're on the flat,

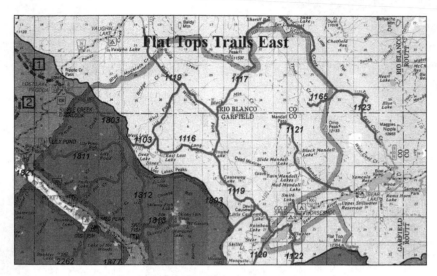

FLAT TOPS TRAILS EAST

you'll enjoy spectacular views of the plateau and its many peaks. From the top, it's only a quarter mile west to Trail 1803 at the White River–Routt National Forest boundary. At the junction, you have several options: continue west to Trappers Lake on Trail 1814, follow Trail 1803 along the Chinese Wall, or hike south to connect with other trails.

NORTH DERBY TRAIL 1122
AND HOOPER LAKE TRAIL 1860

UTM 13 318859 E, 4432761 N
Lat/Lon 40° 1' 38.95" N, 107° 7' 21.94" W

Description In addition to giving access to the head of the Derby Creek drainage, this trail takes you to the base of Flat Top Mountain, the highest point in the Flat Tops Wilderness.

The Derby Creek–Bear River divide, 2 miles south of Stillwater Reservoir, is the boundary of two National Forests: White River and Routt.

Destination Trail 1860, Hooper and Keener Lakes Spur, Edge Lake Trail, Trail 1859, Trail 1842, Stump Park Trailhead

Distance 2.3 miles to Trail 1860, 3.5 miles to Hooper and Keener Lakes Spur, 3.8 miles to Edge Lake Trail, 5.5 miles to Trail 1859, 6 miles to Trail 1842, 9 miles to Stump Park Trailhead

Elevation 10,250 at Stillwater Trailhead; 11,200 on the divide; 10,800 near Hooper and Keener Lakes

Directions to trailhead From Yampa, drive 17 miles west on County Road 7 (this road changes into Forest Road 900 inside the Routt National Forest) to Stillwater Reservoir. Parking is available at the end of the road.

Maps Flat Tops NE

From the parking area go west on the trail for about 110 yards to the junction of Trail 1122. A sign marks the junction. Follow the left fork, which is Trail 1122. (The other is Trail 1119, which follows the north shoreline of Stillwater Reservoir and after 0.7 mile connects with Trail 1120 west of the inlet.)

After crossing the dam, you cross a flat wetland before entering the timber to begin an ascent that will take you above timberline. Trail 1122 begins climbing through spruce and fir forest toward the divide, which is 2.3 miles away and nearly 1,000 feet higher. This divide serves as the boundary between the Routt and White River National Forests.

In places, the climb is rather steep, even on the switchbacks. You pass several small ponds and a trickle of water running downhill,

There aren't many good campsites here. If cattle graze nearby watch where you step. The same goes for sheep.

all near the trail and sources of drinking water. Be sure to treat it, though. The last half mile of the climb is on a steep, rocky path. Footing can be tricky on the loose sand. At the divide, the designation changes to Trail 1860. This divide separates the Colorado and Yampa River drainages.

Views from the divide are overwhelming. To the north, you see the Devils Causeway, the long, northeast-southwest ridge jutting out from the plateau. In the distance to the south, you see the sharp peaks of the Maroon Bells-Snowmass Wilderness Area, south of Interstate 70. There, 2 miles to the east, you see Flat Top Mountain, the tallest peak in the Flat Tops Wilderness at 12,354 feet. The view at the top is worth the hike. On a clear day, visibility exceeds 100 miles.

South of the divide, you cross a grassy knoll to descend into a basin filled with lakes and drained by small streams, the headwaters of Derby Creek. On the west is a high vertical basalt wall, rising to the high knob of 12,186-foot Derby Peak. You'll see a waterfall, depending on the season and amount of remaining snowpack, dropping a few hundred feet off the top, north of the peak.

A half mile down the slope you come to a fork in the trail, marked only by a small pile of rocks. The barely noticeable junction is near a small pond just west of the trail. The west fork passes the outlet of Hooper Lake, which can be seen over a low rise. The lake sits in a bowl below the wall. Keener Lake, the third in a group of four lakes, a quarter mile farther south, is where you connect with a junction of the trail leading to it.

Camping is prohibited within a quarter mile of both Hooper and Keener Lakes. There are meadows nearby but cattle grazing in the area can make it a challenge to find a pleasant location. The lakes are the best water source but you should filter or boil it before drinking.

At the first junction after crossing the knoll, the one mentioned above, the left fork of the trail continues southwest down a grassy slope. In places, the trail fades and is hard to find since it isn't maintained. Just stay in the open between the trees along the west and east sides of the meadow. Be aware that cattle may graze the area, so watch where you step. After descending the short grassy slope, the left fork meets the main Trail 1860 again at the head of a second large, flat meadow.

Back on the main trail, hike another quarter mile to a junction with an undesignated trail bearing to the northeast. This junction is marked with a post. Follow the undesignated trail northeast for 1 mile to Edge Lake.

Return to Trail 1860 and continue south, cross the half-mile-long meadow, and then begin another gradual descent, following the outlet streams from Edge, Hooper, and Keener Lakes. From the Edge Lake trail, continue south almost 2 miles to Trail 1859. Turn north onto Trail 1859 and head uphill for 2 miles to the two Bailey Lakes. Campers staying at Bailey Lakes or Edge Lake must observe the 100-foot restriction.

Take Trail 1859 south back to Trail 1860. A quarter mile southeast past the junction of Trails 1860 and 1859, you connect with Trail 1842. Island Lake Trail 1842 leads west 6.25 miles to Island Lake. Continue south on Trail 1860, which continues its descent southeast passing a few unnamed lakes on the way to the wilderness boundary and Stump Park, a distance of 2 more miles.

EDGE LAKE TRAIL

UTM 13 319941 E, 4428436 N
Lat/Lon 39° 59' 19.86" N, 107° 6' 31.99" W

Description Edge Lake is a long, narrow body of water resting at the bottom of a steep wall 1.5 miles southwest of Flat Top Mountain. The path leaves Trail 1860 at the north end of a large, flat meadow. It heads northeast, wandering around the nose of a timbered ridge, then follows the outlet stream through a second meadow to the lake. You'll find campsites west and south of the lake. The USGS Dome Peak quad shows a trail between Edge and Bailey Lakes but it's not maintained.

Destination Edge Lake

Distance 1 mile

Elevation 10,680 at Trail 1860; 10,910 at Edge Lake

Directions to trail From Yampa, drive 17 miles west on County Road 7 (this road changes into Forest Road 900 inside the Routt National Forest) to Stillwater Reservoir. Parking is available at the end of the road. Four miles from Stillwater Reservoir along Trails 1122 and 1860.

Maps Flat Tops NE

This is an easy 1-mile hike northeast through meadows. It climbs about 250 feet in that distance. Edge Lake, surrounded by timber, is reported to have brook and cutthroat trout.

BAILEY LAKES TRAIL 1859

UTM 13 319943 E, 4428446 N
Lat/Lon 39° 59′ 20.04″ N, 107° 6′ 35.30″ W

Description The path departs from Trail 1860 beside a marshy area and heads north. It follows a moderate slope through the trees a short distance before entering a broad meadow, marshy in spots. The trail crosses the outlet from Bailey Lakes, and then follows the creek across an almost—but not quite—flat woodland. You enter another clearing at the lower lake. You'll see the trail leading through the narrow meadow, which leads to the upper lake. You could also follow the stream to the west between the two lakes. The land around the lakes is reasonably flat, providing for campsites.

The outlet stream a mile south of Bailey Lakes is joined by a second small creek entering from the east. In a meadow, hidden among the timber, are several ponds that could offer secluded campsites.

Destination Bailey Lakes

Distance 2 miles

Elevation 10,310 at Trail 1860; 10,798 at Bailey Lakes

Directions to trail From Stillwater Reservoir, hike south along Trail 1122 (which turns into Trail 1860 at the divide) for 6 miles to the junction with Bailey Lakes Trail 1859.

Maps Flat Tops NE

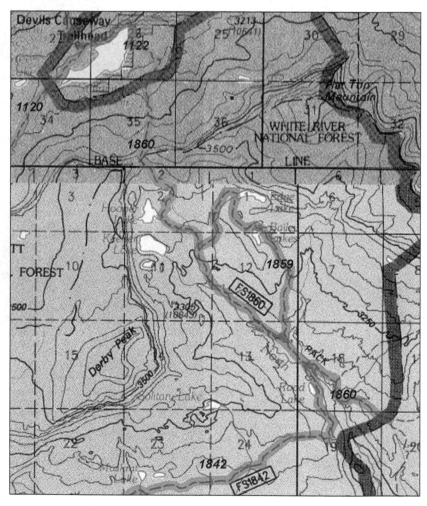

HOOPER, KEENER LAKES

10

EAGLE COUNTY ROAD 301

Eagle County Road 301 turns off to the southwest from State Highway 131 17 miles south of Yampa and 22 miles north of Wolcott. The turn is at the county line and is marked with a sign reading "Burns." After a mile, the road joins the Colorado River, which it follows all the way to Interstate 70, a distance of 36 miles. The Burns Post Office, on the south side of the road, is 12 miles downriver. Just past the Post Office, Eagle County Road 39, also known as the Derby Mesa Loop, heads northwest from Eagle County Road 301.

County Road 39 takes you to Derby Junction and the other end of the Derby Mesa Loop, 1 mile past Burns. From Burns, it's another 15 miles to County Road 40, the Sweetwater Lake Road. The next road, 5.5 miles to the south at Deep Creek, is County Road 17, which becomes Forest Road 600 inside the National Forest boundary. Another 1.5 miles along Eagle County Road 301 takes you to Interstate 70.

EAGLE COUNTY ROAD 39

Just past the Burns Post Office, Eagle County Road 39, also known as the Derby Mesa Loop, heads northwest. Seven miles from Burns, it connects with Forest Road 610. The junction is marked with a sign, "Stump Park Road No. 610."

Drive 2.5 miles farther along Derby Mesa Loop to Forest Road 613, then 5 miles to Derby Junction and return to Eagle County Road 301 at Derby Junction. The last 2 miles of the Loop is steep and winding, giving a great view of the Colorado River below.

FOREST ROAD 610

Eagle County Road 39 connects with Forest Road 610 7 miles from Burns. The junction is marked with a sign, "Stump Park Road No. 610." The first half mile of Forest Road 610 is through private property so you must stay on the road. After passing through a gate, you're on public land. Park here unless you are driving a high clearance four-wheel drive, which is required to travel from the gate to the Stump Park Trailhead.

HOOPER LAKE TRAIL 1860

UTM 13 323523 E, 4424183 N
Lat/Lon 39° 57′ 4,96″ N, 107° 3′ 56.89 W

Description This trail connects with Trail 1122, which is described in the chapter for trails accessed from Routt County Road 7. Reaching the trailhead from Eagle County Road 301 requires four-wheel-drive.

Destination Trail 1842, Trail 1859, Edge Lake Trail, Trail 1122

Distance 2 miles to Trail 1842, 2.7 miles to Trail 1859, 4.4 miles to Edge Lake Trail, 4.8 miles to Hooper/Keener Lakes spur, 6 miles to Trail 1122, 8.3 miles to trailhead of Trail 1119 at Stillwater Reservoir and Forest Road 900

Elevation 9,900 at Stump Park Trailhead; 11,190 at Routt-White River National Forest boundary; 10,260 at trailhead of Trail 1119

Directions to trailhead From Eagle County Road 39, go west on Forest Road 610 4 miles to junction of Forest Road 612. Go northwest, staying on Forest Road 610. From the junction, it's 3 miles to Trail 1860.

Because of short but steep grades, a short wheelbase vehicle will handle the road best. The last mile of road goes through volcanic clay soils, which become extremely greasy with even a light rain. It may be best to stay off this portion of the road when it's wet.

Maps Flat Tops NE

For trail description, see Trails 1122 and 1860, page 172.

ISLAND LAKE TRAIL 1842

UTM 13 321945 E, 4426324 N
Lat/Lon 39° 58′ 12.93″ N, 107° 5′ 5.63″ W

Description This trail gives you a view of three peaks: Dome and Derby Peaks, and Sheep Mountain. It leads across volcanic debris and soils left behind after the glaciers melted. You'll encounter a lot of small ups and downs on this east–west oriented trail. Clay soils will be especially sticky when wet.

The trail connects Trails 1860 on the east and 1816 on the west.

Destination Road Lake, Trail 1846, Trail 1858, Island Lakes, Trail 1857 and Trail 1802, Trail 1817

Distance 0.5 mile to Road Lake, 1.2 miles to Trail 1846, 4.5 miles to Trail 1858, 6 miles to Island Lakes, 6.5 miles to Trails 1857 and 1802, 8 miles to Trail 1817

Elevation 10,120 at Trail 1860; 11,545 at Trail 1817; 11,275 at Trail 1816

Directions to trail From the junction of Eagle County Road 39 and Forest Road 610, go west on Forest Road 610 for 4 miles to junction of Forest Road 612. Go north at this junction, staying on Forest Road 610 for 3 miles to Stump Park Trailhead. Take Trail 1860 north for 3 miles to the junction with Trail 1842.

An alternate approach is Trail 2039 to the west 0.1 mile south of the end of Forest Road 610. This way, it's a little less than 2 miles to Trail 1842. Head east to Trail 1846. From the junction it's 1.25 miles to Solitary Lake.

Maps Flat Tops NE

Trail 1842 from Trail 1860 to Island Lake is a hike of 6.5 miles. In that distance it climbs only about 700 feet, so it's not a difficult hike, except for getting to the trail. Mud and Muskrat Lakes mark the midpoint of the trail. Both are reported to have fish. There are also several unnamed lakes near the trail but no report regarding fish.

SOLITARY LAKE TRAIL 1846

UTM 13 322056 E, 4425002 N
Lat/Lon 39° 57' 29.77" N, 107° 4' 58.69" W

Description This trail leads northwest up a broad, gently sloping ridge. The way is through open meadow, broken occasionally by small stands of timber. Solitary Lake sits alone on a small shelf at the end of your hike. On the wall to the northwest, you'll see Derby Peak, rising to 12,186 feet and the high point of the plateau above you. The best campsites will be found near the timber south of the lake.

Destination Solitary Lake

Distance 1.3 miles

Elevation 10,428 at trailhead; 10,638 at Solitary Lake

Directions to trailhead From the junction of Eagle County Road 39 and Forest Road 610, go west on Forest Road 610 for 4 miles to junction of Forest Road 612. Go north at this junction, staying on Forest Road 610 for 3 miles to Stump Park Trailhead. From Stump Park go north on Trail 1860 2 miles to junction of Trail 1842. Turn west on Trail 1842 and hike 1.2 miles to the Solitary Lake Trail 1846.

Alternate Route: From the Stump Park Trailhead take Trail 2039 2 miles north to Trail 1842. Go east on Trail 1842 for 0.6 mile to the junction of Trail 1846.

Maps Flat Tops NE

Trail 1846 goes northeast over open terrain over a gentle slope that climbs 200 feet between Trail 1842 and Solitary Lake. Open country with a few scattered patches of trees. Good sites to camp around the lake in the open areas, or the timber on the west end of Solitary.

MIDDLE DERBY TRAIL 1858

UTM 13 324156 E, 4421517 N
Lat/Lon 39° 55' 38.63" N, 107° 3' 26.58" W

Description The trail generally follows the Middle Fork of Derby Creek. The ascent is gradual; not a difficult hike.

Destination McMillan Lake, Trail 2076, Trail 1842

Distance 2 miles to McMillan Lake, 2.6 miles to Trail 2076, 5.5 miles to Trail 1842

Elevation 8,800 at trailhead; 10,103 at Trail 1842

Directions to trailhead From the junction of Eagle County Road 39 and Forest Road 610, turn west on Forest Road 610 and drive 4 miles to junction of Forest Road 612. Go northwest on Forest Road 612. From that junction, it's 1 rough mile to the Middle Derby Trailhead and Trail 1858.

Maps Flat Tops NE

The trail begins by following the Middle Fork of Derby Creek on the way to McMillan Lake. From the trailhead, it's a half mile to the wilderness boundary, 2 miles to McMillan Lake.

From McMillan Lake, continue west 1 mile along Derby Creek on Trail 1858 to the junction of Trail 2076. This trail gives another access point to the wilderness and Trail 1858. Hiking past this junction, the gradual climb continues, leading you through a small canyon, wooded on the south side and bare on the north. Three miles past the trail junction, you connect with Trail 1842. As you get closer to 1842, notice the moraines along the sides of the stream valley. These are the elongated piles of rubble left behind when the glaciers receded as they melted.

At Trail 1842, you can hike east to Island Lake, or east to link up with Trail 1860.

Hiking the Southeast Flat
Tops Forest Road 613

From Derby Junction, drive west on the Derby Mesa Loop for 9.5 miles to the connection with Forest Road 613. Turn west onto Forest Road 613, through the gate. Four-wheel drive is required for roads in this area. The first 1.5 miles is quite rough as it wanders across hard sandstone, which resists weathering. The road takes you through an area burned in June 1980. The Emerald Lake fire destroyed more than 10,000 acres. The biggest forest fire in Colorado was fought by some 500 firefighters. Smoke was visible as far away as Nebraska. Many standing dead trees remain in the burn area. It has since grown up in aspen. On the trip out, the view to the east is great. You have a view of the mountains all the way to the Continental Divide.

The next section of Forest Road 613, which takes you to the South Fork of Derby Creek, goes over limestone in the Morrison Formation and is not quite so rough. Past Deer Park, a long, narrow meadow, the road is rough but not real bad. West from Derby Junction 10.2 miles you come to Forest Road 616. Continue driving west on Forest Road 616, where you descend into the South Fork of Derby Creek 12 miles west from Derby Junction. Ahead to the west, you see Sheep Mountain and its 12,241-foot summit.

Then, you descend a steep, loose, rocky, rough, and bumpy road.

At the bottom, you must ford the South Fork. The crossing is good and solid but the approach is steep leading into the water. A high clearance four-wheel drive is required, preferably one with a short wheelbase. From here, the road gets bad.

Thirteen miles from Derby Junction you come to Trail 2076. In this area Forest Road 613 is nothing more than tracks through the volcanic debris and clay soils. As long as it's dry, travel is only slow going. The challenge comes when it rains and the ground turns to slime, offering little for traction.

Forest Road 613 is extremely popular with local four-wheel-drive enthusiasts and horse users. There is a trailhead just off the Derby Road for those who want to hike from there. Be aware that the road leads through a very narrow corridor surrounded by wilderness where off-road travel is prohibited. The road ends at Mackinaw Lake 18 miles from Derby Junction. From there, travel into the wilderness is by foot or pack animal only.

You may wonder if the drive to Mackinaw Lake is worth the effort. That depends. It will save several miles of hiking if the Island Lakes or Deer Lake is your destination.

ROBERTS TRAIL 2076

UTM 13 321450 E, 4418682 N
Lat/Lon 39° 54' 4.46" N, 107° 5' 19.6" W

Description This is a short hike that follows the wilderness boundary north to Trail 1858.

Destination Trail 1858

Distance 3.5 miles

Elevation 9,460 at Forest Road 613 and Trail 2076; 10,100 halfway to Trail 1858; 9,383 at Trail 1858

Directions to trailhead From the junction of Eagle County Road 39

(Derby Mesa Loop) and Forest Road 613, go west on Forest Road 613, 8 miles to the trail. Four-wheel drive is needed.

Maps Flat Tops NE

This trail provides another way into the wilderness in the Middle Fork of Derby Creek area. From the sign at the trailhead, your walk begins as an easy climb through the trees. Midway along Trail 2076 (about 1.5 miles from the trailhead) is a spur leading to the west and the base of Sheep Mountain. This spur ends at a small pothole. Should you want to ascend the peak, you'll need to use map and compass to navigate through the timber to reach an open slope that you can take to the summit. The route gets steep but is nontechnical.

Head back to the main trail that continues north past this spur through a spruce forest and small clearings. Past the last meadow, the trail turns toward the east and descends along the nose of a ridge, avoiding the much steeper slope just around the corner to the west. You connect with Trail 1858 at the wilderness boundary.

SOUTH DERBY TRAIL 1857

UTM 13 315473 E, 4419818 N
Lat/Lon 39° 54′ 36.56″ N, 107° 9′ 31.62″ W

Description This trail offers a short walk onto the plateau but only if your vehicle can handle the road. The path climbs fast, and for a short distance it ascends a very steep wall, using switchbacks.

Destination Island Lakes, Trail 1842, Trail 1802

Distance 2.1 miles to Island Lakes, 2.5 miles to Trail 1842, 2.6 miles to Trail 1802

Elevation 10,778 at Mackinaw Lake; 11,200 at Upper Island Lake

Directions to trailhead From the junction of Eagle County Road 39 and Forest Road 613, go west on Forest Road 613 for 12 miles to Crescent Lake and the trailhead. This road to the trailhead is challenging, very rough and rocky. Park at the end of the road near Mackinaw Lake.

Maps Flat Tops NE

The trail begins between Crescent and Mackinaw Lakes at the bottom of a glacially carved gorge. Northeast of the lakes are several unnamed pothole lakes, scattered across the hummocky terrain, left behind when the sheet of ice melted.

Begin by hiking north on Trail 1857 along the east shore of Mackinaw (the west lake). Beyond the lake you begin a gradual climb that becomes radically steeper as you ascend the wall of the gorge. Switchbacks make the short ascent somewhat easier. Once on top, you see Upper Island Lake and several small potholes on the flat, west of Upper Island Lake. Look back to the east to see scattered ponds on the timbered flat northeast of Mackinaw Lake. From the top, it's less than a half mile west along Trail 1857 to the junction with Trail 1842. You can also see Island Lake, 300 feet below your boots to the north. Turn northeast on Trail 1842 and hike a half mile to Island Lake. This is the easiest route to the lake, which has suitable campsites in the timber along the north shore. The Island Lakes have cutthroats.

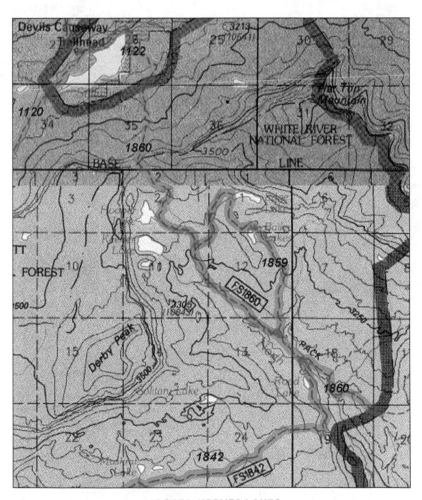

HOOPER, KEENER LAKES

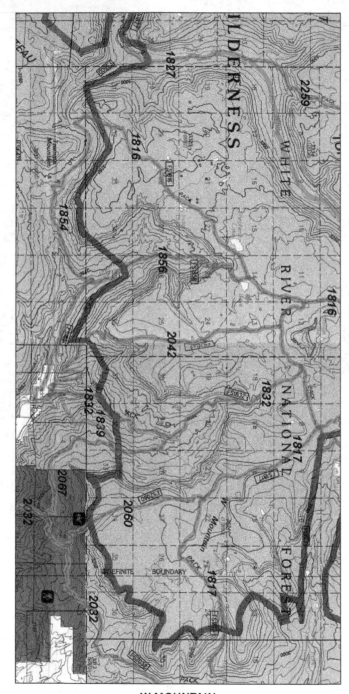

W MOUNTAIN

TURRET–CRESCENT TRAIL 2269

UTM 13 315928 E, 4419485 N
Lat/Lon 39° 54′ 26.29″ N, 107° 9′ 11.51″ W

Description This climb is much less severe than Trail 1857. Once on top, you'll cross the nearly level plateau in the shadow of Shingle Peak.

Destination Trail 1817, Trail 1832 and Shingle Peak

Distance 2 miles to Trail 1817, 3 miles to Trail 1832 and Shingle Peak

Elevation 10,760 at Mackinaw Lake; 11,446 at Trail 1817; 11,222 at Trail 1832

Directions to trailhead From the junction of Eagle County Road 39 and Forest Road 613, go west on Forest Road 613 12 miles to Crescent Lake and the trailhead. Park at east end of Crescent Lake

Map Flat Tops NE

This is another trail accessed from the Crescent Lake Road (Forest Road 613). It gets you onto the Flat Tops a little quicker than the other route, Trail 1857. Follow the posted signs at the trailhead to begin Trail 2269. It's about 1.5 miles from Crescent Lake to the top of the flat and the junction with Trail 1817.

Once up on the flat, you see dozens of potholes east of Shingle Peak. The 1.5-mile walk past the lakes is high meadow, with only scattered stands of timber on the plateau. Straight west is Shingle Peak, a massive basaltic mountain having horizontal and vertical fractures giving it the appearance of a shingled roof when the light is just right. Sunrise or sunset, when the light plays off the peak, accentuating the dull red tones of the eroding basalt, are the two best times to view the mountain.

Just east of the peak on the flat, the trail connects with Trail 1832. Follow the trail west along the south side of Shingle Peak. Going south on 1832 will take you down Turret Creek to Sweetwater Lake.

FOREST ROAD 616

This road goes south from Forest Road 613 4 miles past the Derby Loop Road. It has the same problems as Forest Road 613 as it travels across volcanic rubble and clay soils, so you will need a high clearance four-wheel-drive vehicle. It's not quite 2 miles to the end of the road and the W Mountain Trailhead.

W MOUNTAIN TRAIL 1817

UTM 13 323032 E, 4415549 N
Lat/Lon 39° 52' 25" N, 107° 4' 10" W

Description W Mountain is the one with the distinctive east face you see from State Highway 131. As its name suggest, it appears as the letter *W*. The feature is more easily noticed in the early spring, when there's still snow on the plateau.

Most of the climb on this trail occurs in the first 3 miles. Once up on the plateau, hiking is much easier. Carry plenty of water.

Destination W Mountain and Trail 2060, Trail 2269, Trail 1842

Distance 5.25 miles to W Mountain and Trail 2060, 8.5 miles north to Trail 2269, 10.25 miles to Trail 1842

Elevation 9,596 at W Mountain Trailhead; 11,500 at Trail 1917

Directions to trailhead From the junction of Eagle County Road 39 and Forest Road 613 5 miles to the junction of Forest Road 616. Go left (south) on Forest Road 616 and drive 2 miles to the trailhead. The road takes you through an area burned in the summer of 1979. As with other roads in this area, you must contend with volcanic rubble and soils to reach this trailhead. Park at the end of the road west of Big Spring. This is also the trailhead for Trail 2032 that goes south, east of the wilderness area.

Maps Flat Tops NE

It is advisable to carry plenty of water on this trail. There are several stretches where none is available. The trail begins at the end of Forest Road 616 at a place called Big Spring. It heads west up a moderate slope before turning to traverse the grade. From there it generally follows a small canyon above an unnamed creek. The trail continues climbing, but the ascent is gradual except in a couple of places near the head of the canyon.

W Mountain is not really a definable peak but more of a high point along the rim. When you reach the top of the plateau, look to the north where you see a 200-foot rampart. Buck and Star Lakes are just below this point. They're about a half mile off the trail. There is no path leading to the lakes.

On top, Trail 1817 meanders through a high open meadow, climbing gradually to cross W Mountain. From here, you cross to the west side of the high ridge to overlook a glacially scoured drainage 1,300 feet below. The trail heads north along a narrowing ridge past the 11,850-foot summit of the very broad W Mountain. The high point of the trail is a half mile farther north at 11,739 feet. Look east here to view Bull Lake, nearly 800 feet below.

Another mile along the trail brings you to Trail 2269. To the west of this intersection, you'll get a look at Shingle Peak. Hike north past the trail junction and pass the head of the South Fork of Derby Creek. Near the head of this glacial valley can be seen Crescent and Mackinaw Lakes.

Two miles north of the junction with Trail 2269 is the junction with Trail 1842. Trail 1842 leads east past the two Island Lakes. Beyond the intersection with Trail 1842, the main Trail 1817 wanders along the basaltic plateau below a long, low, north-trending hill to the east. After another mile the trail heads west to connect with Trail 1816. You can go north on this trail to Trappers Lake.

SOUTH W MOUNTAIN TRAIL 2060

UTM 13 316586 E, 4414962 N
Lat/Lon 39° 52' 0.77" N, 107° 8' 40.35" W

Description Southwest of W Mountain, this trail heads south to connect with Trail 2032. It departs from the W Mountain Trail at the south end of a willow grove. As on Trail 1817, the hike is across the treeless plateau until you reach the head of the West Fork of Sheep Creek.

Destination Trail 2032

Distance 3.75 miles

Elevation 11,500 at Trail 1817; 10,110 at Trail 2032

Directions to trail From the junction of Eagle County Road 39 and Forest Road 613 5 miles to the junction of Forest Road 616. Go left (south) on Forest Road 616 and drive 2 miles to the trailhead. The road takes you through an area burned in the summer of 1979. As with other roads in this area, you must contend with volcanic rubble and soils to reach this trailhead. Park at the end of the road west of Big Spring. This is also the trailhead for Trail 2032 that goes south, east of the wilderness area. From the Big Spring Trailhead, hike 4 miles west on Trail 1817 to the junction with Trail 2060.

Alternatively, from the junction of Trails 1817 and 2269, hike 3 miles south on Trail 1817 to connect with 2060.

Map Flat Tops NE

The first mile of your walk on Trail 2060 is through a grove of willows as the trail follows the west side of the uniquely shaped mountain. Below to the west, the sides of the plateau get steeper, becoming nearly vertical, dropping away more than a thousand feet to the wooded slopes below.

Near the head of the West Fork of Sheep Creek 2 miles along the trail, the route begins a descent. The head of the drainage is broad but as you hike downward, the sides close in. The path follows the west side of the valley, taking you down the nose of a narrow, timber-covered ridge for a ways, using switchbacks to keep the grade moderate. At the bottom of the descent, the slope flattens. Here, you connect with Trail 2032. Continuing past this junction it's 6.5 miles to the trailhead of Trail 1817.

11

EAGLE COUNTY ROAD 301 (COLORADO RIVER ROAD)

From State Highway 131, 28 miles south on Eagle County Road 301 to Eagle County Road 40. Turn right (west) on Eagle County Road 40. It's 7 miles along this gravel road to the Garfield County line, where the designation changes to Garfield County Road 150. From there, it's 3 miles to Sweetwater Lake, then 2 more miles to the end of the road.

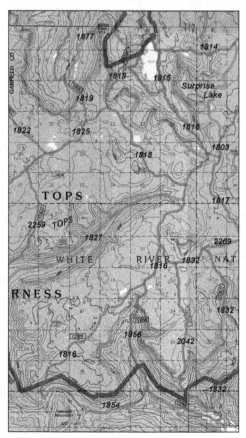

SURPRISE LAKE

TURRET CREEK TRAIL 1832

UTM 13 313117 E, 4409308 N
Lat/Lon 39° 48' 54.64" N, 107° 10' 59.67" W

Description This trail follows Turret Creek. You're going uphill all the way to Shingle Peak, 8 miles away. For the climb, you stay close to the creek so water won't be a problem. A mile from the trailhead, Trail 1839 goes east to connect with Trail 2067 a half mile south of the wilderness boundary.

Destination Trail 1854, Trail 2042, Trail 2067, Trail 2269, Trail 1816

Distance 0.4 mile to Trail 1854, 0.6 mile to Trail 2042, 3.7 miles to Trail 2067, 7.7 miles to Trail 2269, 10 miles to Trail 1816

Elevation 8,000 at Turret Creek Trailhead; 11,222 at the junction of Trails 1832 and 2269

Directions to trailhead From County Road 301 (Colorado River Road) drive west on Eagle County Road 40 for 12 miles, and continue past Sweetwater Lake to end of the road. Unless you have four-wheel drive, park at the bottom of the steep grade in the small marked area by the road.

Map Flat Tops NE

This trail gains a total of 3,200 feet. It begins in scrub oak brush. The first mile of Trail 1832 is through private property so stay on the trail. After going around the end of a ridge, you skirt the edge of the timber as you ascend the narrow canyon drained by Turret Creek. In the first 2 miles, you climb a thousand feet. The next 2 miles takes you up another 800 feet, where you emerge from the trees into Turret Creek Meadows, a half-mile-long opening. Expect to find an abundance of wildflowers here in early summer.

The trail passes the meadow along the west side, where you begin another ascent in the shadow of 11,525-foot Turret Peak. The peak isn't large. It's a cone-shaped mountain, timbered all the way to the top. The east face, though, is a sharp drop-off, falling away more than 600 feet. Over the next mile, you pass in and out of the timber in sight of the tiny creek. When you break into the open for the last short ascent, you have a view of a falls dropping nearly 40 feet.

The gradient is gentle as you approach Shingle Peak from the south. Hiking 1.5 miles past the falls, you connect with Trail 2269 below the peak.

Over the next 2 miles, the trail wanders through the high tundra below the basaltic mountain. After a mile, you reach the northern terminus of Trail 2042. Be aware that the USFS trail information and Trails Illustrated Flat Tops NE map disagree on the end of Trail 1832. Continuing to the northeast you connect with Trail 1816, which leads to Trappers Lake.

JOHNNY MEYERS LAKE TRAIL 2067

UTM 13 314546 E, 4413903 N
Lat/Lon 39° 51′ 24,35″ N, 107° 10′ 4.58″ W

Description This trail takes you to Johnny Meyers Lake, at the wilderness boundary. The route leads through the wooded slope seen from the plateau near W Mountain. While the ground is rough and uneven, the elevation varies little.

Destination Trail 1839, Trail 2032

Distance 1.5 miles to Trail 1839, 5 miles to Trail 2032

Elevation 9,600 at Trail 1832; 10,060 1 mile west of Hack Lake; 9,800 at Trail 2032

Directions to trail From County Road 301 (Colorado River Road) drive west on Eagle County Road 40 for 12 miles, and continue past Sweetwater Lake to end of the road. Unless you have four-wheel drive, park at bottom of the steep grade in the small marked area by the road. From the Turret Creek Trailhead, Trail 1832 connects with Trail 2067 after climbing 3.7 miles above Turret Creek. At the trail junction, you can hike 2 miles south on Trail 2607 to reach Johnny Meyer Lake.

Maps Flat Tops NE

SHINGLE PEAK TRAIL 2042

UTM 13 313117 E, 4409308 N
Lat/Lon 39° 48′ 54.64″ N, 107° 10′ 59.67″ W

Description This is a trail that will test your heart, lungs, and legs. It climbs 2,600 feet in the first 4 miles. Once you reach the plateau, the hike is nearly flat over the next 3 miles to Trail 1832. Water is scarce on this trail.

Destination Trail 1832

Distance 7 miles

Elevation 8,000 at Turret Creek Trailhead; 11,222 at Trail 1832 southeast of Shingle Peak

Directions to trail From County Road 301 (Colorado River Road) drive west on Eagle County Road 40 for 12 miles, and continue past Sweetwater Lake to end of the road and the Turret Creek Trailhead. Unless you have four-wheel drive, park at bottom of the steep grade in the small marked area by the road. From Trail 1832, 3.7 miles from the Turret Creek Trailhead above Sweetwater Lake, hike west one-half mile on Trail 1854 to junction of Trail 1832. Follow Trail 1832 around the ridge to the first trail that heads west; this is Trail 2042 and it heads west up the steep slope.

Maps Flat Tops NE

Trail 2042 is the second junction along Trail 1832, a half mile past the Turret Creek Trailhead. It begins on an open slope, climbing the nose of the ridge, using switchbacks to get you up the slope. After passing the first opening in the timber, you reach a junction in the trail. To the right is a trail connecting to Trail 1832 and Turret Creek. Go left to stay on Trail 2042.

At the second opening on the ridge, the trail swings left, returning to the nose of the ridge to continue upward. You reach the plateau 2 miles farther north. At that point, you have ascended 2,600 feet in only 4 miles.

On the flat, you still climb, but the gradient is much lower, nearly unnoticeable. After 2.5 miles of meandering through timber and open parks, you reach a fork in the trail. The left fork takes you to Rim Lake and Trails 1856 and 1816. Trail 2042 goes right here. Near the fork is a pond and a spring. This is the first water source since leaving the trailhead 5 miles back. You come to Trail 1832 at the base of Shingle Peak 1.5 miles past the fork.

RIM LAKE TRAIL 1856

UTM 13 309030 E, 4411322 N
Lat/Lon 39° 49' 56.54" N, 107° 13' 53.69" W

Description As is typical of the trails on the southeast side of the plateau, this one climbs rapidly. It follows Sweetwater Creek to its source, so water isn't a problem. The path stays at the bottom of the draw until you near the headwall of the canyon, where it climbs out rather sharply.

Destination Rim Lake, Trail 1816

Distance 5 miles to Rim Lake and 5 miles to Trail 1816

Elevation 8,530 at Trail 1854; 10,826 at Trail 1816

Directions to trail From County Road 301 (Colorado River Road) drive west on Eagle County Road 40 for 12 miles, and continue past Sweetwater Lake to end of the road. Unless you have four-wheel drive, park at bottom of the steep grade in the small marked area by the road. From the Turret Creek Trailhead, 3 miles west on Trail 1854 to the junction with Trail 1856.

Alternate Access to Shepherd and Rim Lakes From Forest Road 600 to Trappers Lake Trail 1816 at Indian Camp Pass, page 207–9. This is an easier route.

The upper Sweetwater Creek drainage descends a steep, rugged, glacially scoured canyon. From Trail 1854, the bottom of the canyon is nearly flat and broad. A mile north and just across the wilderness boundary, the stream drains through a large boggy area. The trail keeps to the higher ground east of the swamp, where it begins climbing across a steep, rocky, open slope. Here, the ascent becomes steeper, leading onto a small ledge where you can take a breather.

Trail 1856 crosses the creek a short distance farther, then begins another steady climb. You cross a second open slope, and then skirt a grove of low brush before crossing Sweetwater Creek again. From this point, the climb becomes serious. You work your way up and around a steep slope covered with slide rock. If you look up the fork of the creek coming from the northwest, you'll see a series of falls as the stream tumbles down the nearly vertical wall. Take a break and dig out your camera before continuing on. Also, remember that you have less than a mile to go to reach the plateau.

Near the top of the canyon, the trail makes a turn to the east and follows a gentler slope along Sweetwater Creek. You break out into the open almost in sight of Rim Lake, aptly named for its position on the edge of the plateau. Past the lake, 0.1 mile north, you connect with Trail 1816. Here, you can go left and descend to Indian Camp Pass, or go north to Trappers Lake.

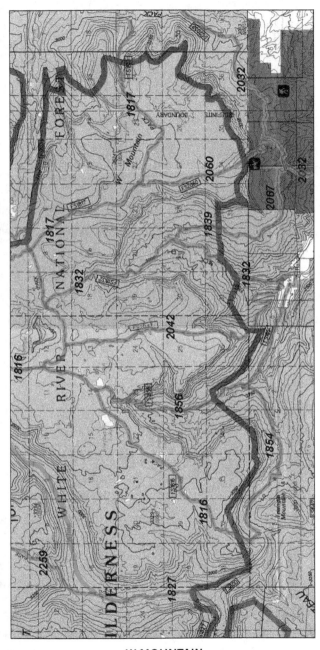

W MOUNTAIN

12

FOREST ROAD 600

Eagle County Road 17, at Deep Creek, leaves Eagle County Road 301 34 miles south from State Highway 131, and 1.5 miles north from Interstate 70. After crossing the National Forest boundary, Eagle County Road 17 changes to Forest Road 600. Fourteen miles from County Road 301 is a spur to the north leading to the Deep Creek Overlook. At 18 miles, you come to Broken Rib Spring, a good source of water. Forest Road 601, leading west to Heart Lake, is 29 miles from Eagle County Road 301. Another mile along Forest Road 600 takes you to Deep Lake. The road this far is narrow but in good condition.

From Deep Lake, it's 5 miles to Indian Camp Pass, then 3 more miles to the Meadows, and another mile to Budge's Flattops Wilderness Lodge and the end of the road, a distance of 39 miles from County Road 301. Allow about two hours to drive the entire distance. Drivers of vehicles with low clearance should not go much past Deep Lake. All other roads in the area are environmentally challenged—very rough.

DEEP CREEK OVERLOOK

You hear the roar of Deep Creek, subdued by the 2,300-foot drop below the limestone rim. From the overlook on the south rim, you can look across to the other side and see caves in the limestone wall. The deep gorge is another feature found on the Flat Tops created by the sheet of ice that covered the region a few thousand years ago.

Most visitors are satisfied to simply stop and look upon this magnificent vista, a sight unequaled elsewhere in the wilderness. For the adventurous, game trails lead down the vertical sides into the depths of the gorge.

The Overlook provides a magnificent vista of Deep Creek a half mile below the canyon rim.

The overlook is on Forest Road 600, 14 miles from Eagle County Road 301. The spur road is marked with a sign reading "Deep Creek Overlook." Park at the end of the road and walk over to the rim. A chain-link fence protects you from the severe exposure. Camping is not permitted in the immediate area.

TRAPPERS LAKE TRAIL 1816

UTM 13 303601 E, 4410847 N
Lat/Lon 39° 49′ 36.82 N, 107° 17′ 41.74″ W

Description This one traverses the wilderness from south to north, eventually taking you to Trappers Lake. You climb a thousand feet in the first 1.5 miles but once on top, the hike is easy.

Destination Indian Lake, Shepherd Lake, Trail 1856, Rim Lake, Trail 2269, Trail 1818, Trail 1817, Trail 1815

Distance 3 miles to Indian Lake, 5.1 miles to Shepherd Lake, 6 miles to Trail 1856, 7.4 miles to Rim Lake, 10.8 miles to Trail 1832, 11.8 miles to Trail 1818, 13 miles to Trail 1817, 15.4 miles to Trail 1815

Elevation 9,724 at Indian Camp Pass; 11,125 at Trail 1832

Directions to trailhead From the junction of Eagle County Road 301 and Forest Road 600, drive north 35 miles to Indian Camp Pass and the trailhead. Trail 1816 ascends the slope directly to the north. This is also the west trailhead of Trail 1854, which follows the canyon to the east, ending at the Sweetwater Trailhead.

Maps Flat Tops NE

From the trailhead, the climb is steady as you ascend the slope to the plateau. It cuts across the slope, though, so it isn't too bad a climb. You top out on the plateau where the grade is much gentler as you head northeast. At 2 miles, the way is nearly level and you make good time across the wooded flat. Interspersed with the trees are broad open expanses of green meadows.

You pass a few pothole lakes on the way to Indian Lake, 3 miles from the start of your hike, beside the trail. Another 2 miles takes you to Shepherd Lake on the west side of the trail. It lies in a broad opening. The timber on the south side is suitable for camping.

Past the crossing of the outlet stream from Shepherd Lake 0.6 mile, you connect with Trail 1856 (Trail 1856 comes in from the south, up a fork of Sweetwater Creek).

At the junction of Trails 1816 and 1856 you can see Rim Lake. It sits at the head of the canyon drained by Sweetwater Creek and is the stream's source. It's out in the open. The tallest vegetation around it are the willows that crowd the shoreline in places.

From either Shepherd Lake or Rim Lake, your view of 11,996-foot Shingle Peak to the northeast is unobstructed. The peak is one of the remnants of the volcanism that covered the Flat Tops over the past seventy million years. It rises only about 800 feet above the plateau but is impressive due to its massive size. This basaltic mountain is appropriately named as the fracture pattern in the rock and its color at sunset causes it to appear as the roof of a giant's barn, covered with red shingles. You'll get the best photos of the peak at sunset from the west side.

As you travel north, Trail 1816 leads past several small pothole lakes scattered about the plateau. Two miles past Rim Lake, you'll connect with Trail 2269 due west of Shingle Peak. This trail will take you east to the Shingle Peak, Turret Creek, and W Mountain Trails.

Pass by the junction with Trail 1832 and for the next 2 miles Trail 1816 is through high meadows below and west of the peak. Two miles from the junction with Trail 1832 you cross the outlet of Shingle Lake. The lake sits on a shelf below the north slope of Shingle Peak a mile south of the trail. No path leads to it, but by following the stream you'll find it all right.

The stream exiting Shingle Lake is one of several that form the headwaters of the South Fork of the White River. At the creek, you can look below and see the river flowing southwest at the bottom of an 800-foot gorge. The South Fork Trail 1827 follows the stream down to the Meadows. The trail is not maintained until the confluence of Doe Creek so it may be hard to find.

If you stay on Trail 1816, a mile north of the Shingle Lake outlet stream you cross the main branch of the South Fork's headwaters.

The water collects in a cluster of potholes scattered about the plateau to the north. Continuing north another quarter mile, you connect with Trail 1818, which leads 2 miles to Wall Lake and Trappers Peak to the west.

The flat to the north and west of the trail junction is covered with pothole lakes, the headwaters of the South Fork of the White River. One note of interest here is that both forks of the White River head in this area within a mile of each other.

About a mile past Trail 1818, you come to the junction of Trail 1842, which leads east 2.5 miles to Island Lake and the W Mountain Trail. At this junction, Trail 1816 begins a rapid descent on the way down the glacial valley leading to Trappers Lake. Near the head of the valley 1 mile down the trail from the plateau, you pass within a short distance of Parvin Lake, located in a cirque below the west wall. You should be able to find campsites on the flats north and south of the lake.

Past Parvin Lake, the descent becomes more gradual, almost flat in places in the next 3 miles, where you connect with Trail 1815, the one that takes you around the shoreline of Trappers Lake. Going west

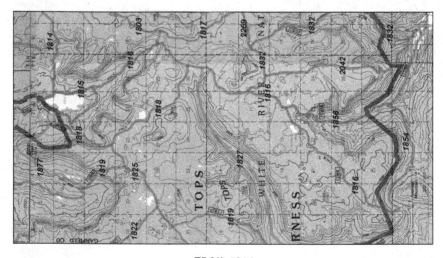

TRAIL 1816

onto Trail 1815 at the junction will take you to the Scotts Bay Trail Head, a distance of 2 miles if you follow the lakeshore. Taking the right fork leads north to Trail 1814. Follow it north past the CPW cabins to the Outlet Trailhead.

WAGONWHEEL CREEK TRAIL 2049

UTM 13 297894 E, 4406554 N
Lat/Lon 39° 47' 12.37" N, 107° 21' 36.53" W

Description This trail is an easy walk through a beautiful stream plain. The last 1.5 miles take you down the nose of a ridge to Budge's Flattops Wilderness Lodge. You can hike it from either end. This trail is a good one to ride if you're staying at Budge's. With horses, you could make a long trip by following this one south, and then go over to Patterson Creek Trailhead—this could be a good one- or two-night trail ride.

Destination South Fork of the White River and Budge's Flattops Wilderness Lodge

Distance 5 miles

Elevation 10,770 at Forest Road 640 and Trail 2049; 9,038 at Budge's Flattops Wilderness Lodge

Directions to trailhead West on Eagle County Road 17 at Deep Creek, which becomes Forest Road 600 at the National Forest boundary. Drive 29 miles on Forest Road 600 to Forest Road 601. A sign at the junction reads, "Heart Lake 1 mile." Turn west on Forest Road 601.

High-clearance four-wheel drive is required on the following roads. At 0.6 mile, bear left by Klines Folly Campground to Bison Lake. Continue west to Supply Basin Campground. Another 0.9 mile beyond the campground you'll reach the junction with Forest Road 640. Go west on Forest Road 640 for 3.4 miles (past Heart Lake and past Bison Lake) to the junction of Forest Road 645. Go north on Forest Road 645 and drive 1.6 miles to the junction with Forest Road 644, the Dry Buck Loop. Go north at junction onto Dry Buck Loop and drive 0.6 mile to the unmarked trailhead above Wagonwheel Creek. High-clearance four-wheel drive is required on Forest Road 645 and Forest Road 644.

Maps Flat Tops SE, Flat Tops NE

The trailhead is at the end of the Forest Road 644. The trail is a former two-track road, barely visible because the land is successfully reclaiming it. This trail wanders north into the wilderness, following Wagonwheel Creek, a tiny, clear stream flowing over a bed of limestone cobbles. It takes the hunter into good areas for deer and elk that don't require horses to access.

The remnants of beaver ponds can be seen a half mile north along the creek, now broken and no longer maintained since the beavers left. From a limestone rim a quarter mile north of the trailhead, your view across the large meadow is unhindered.

You have several options for hiking in this area. About 1 mile northwest from the trailhead, past the marshy, beaver pond meadow, the trail splits into three branches. The left fork continues on northwest, and then bends around toward the south. You can follow this fork 3 miles to Forest Road 640. The first half of the trail takes you through open parks along stands of pine and spruce forests. The hike is nearly level. The second half begins at a stream crossing, a fork of

Patterson Creek to the west. When you reach Forest Road 640, you can return the same way or follow the road east to Wagonwheel Creek, and then follow the stream cross-country downstream to the trailhead. The stream runs through meadowland, following the wilderness boundary.

The right fork heads east, taking you to Forest Road 644. The path leads through meadows and along the edge of woodlands in the 1.5 miles to the road. At the road, head south for about 1 mile to return to the trailhead.

The third (center) fork is the continuation of the main Trail 2049. It continues north in sight of Wagonwheel Creek. Rock cairns mark the trail through the meadow. After 1.5 miles, the path descends the nose of a ridge, which becomes steeper as you get lower. It ends at Budge's Flattops Wilderness Lodge, 7 miles from the Wagonwheel Trailhead.

BLAIR LAKE TRAIL 2098

UTM 13 293257 E, 4404464 N
Lat/Lon 39° 46′ 0.99″ N, 107° 24′ 48.94″ W

Description This route takes you into a scenic, less used part of the wilderness. The trail is an easy walk with the exception of the climb near Crater Lake. Shadow and Blair Lakes are a challenge to reach off the trail.

Destination Jet Lake, Shadow Lake, Blair Lake, Crater Lake, Crater Lake Trailhead

Distance 2.25 miles to Jet Lake, 3 miles to Shadow Lake, 3.25 miles to Blair Lake, 5 miles to Crater Lake, 7.7 miles to Crater Lake Trailhead

Elevation 10,390 at the trailhead; 11,100 at the trailhead above Crater Lake (descends to 9,960 east of Crater Lake)

Directions to trailhead The southwest area of the Flat Tops is a place having some of the most challenging roads you'll drive. Few are steep but they are exceedingly rough, requiring high-clearance four-wheel-drive vehicles to bounce over boulders and work your way through bogs. The roads are rough enough that you can often walk just as quickly as drive. A four-wheel drive will save you a few miles of carrying a pack though. Carry a high-lift jack or a winch and travel with two vehicles when possible. This may not be essential but it will ease the job of extracting a stuck or high-centered vehicle.

• **Patterson Creek Trailhead** West on Eagle County Road 17 at Deep Creek, which becomes Forest Road 600 at the National Forest boundary. Drive 29 miles on Forest Road 600 to Forest Road 640. From Forest Road 600 heading west all roads require four-wheel drive because of the rough roads, large rocks, and mud when wet. A sign at the junction reads, "Heart Lake 1 mile." Turn west on Forest Road 640. At 0.6 mile, bear left by Klines Folly Campground to Bison Lake. Continue 0.5 mile to Supply Basin Campground. Another 0.9 mile beyond the campground you'll reach the junction with Forest Road 645. Go west on Forest Road 640 for 3.4 miles (past Heart Lake and past Bison Lake) to the junction of Forest Road 645. Go west at the junction to stay on Forest Road 640. It's 5 miles west over a very rough road on Forest Road 640 to Elk Lakes and the trailhead. Park at trailhead. Four-wheel drive is needed.

• **Crater Lake Trailhead** From Buford, head south on Rio Blanco County Road 17 toward New Castle. Note that inside the National

Forest, Rio Blanco County Road 17 becomes Forest Road 245. Eleven miles from Buford, turn east at Hiner Spring on Forest Road 601 (County Road 125). You'll need four-wheel drive on Forest Road 601. Drive 8.5 miles east on Forest Road 601 to the junction with County Road 281. Go east on Forest Road 601 (County Road 281) 7 miles to connect with Forest Road 640. Drive a half mile to the trailhead and park at the Elk Lakes. From the parking area hike north on Trail 2098, Jet, Blair, and Crater Lakes.

Maps Flat Tops NE, Flat Tops SE, Flat Tops SW

Once you've arrived at the trailhead, the hike is easy. From the Patterson Creek Trailhead, head north along an old road leading to the wilderness boundary a half mile away. The first mile is through an open flat. To the west, you see the vertical limestone cliff face of Blair Mountain, which you follow for the length of the trail.

Above the timbered slope to the west and below the cliff is an unnamed lake. No trail leads to it. Expect downed timber on the way.

As you continue north, Trail 2098 takes you through timber and scattered openings. After 2 miles, you pass along the east shore of Jet Lake. A mile north of Jet Lake, the trail passes below a short but steep timbered cliff. Above it lie Shadow and Blair Lakes. Reaching them requires bushwhacking through downed timber up the steep climb. If you want to get to these lakes, the easiest way may be from between Jet and Shadow Lakes—it will require navigating by map and compass, but the slope is much easier.

Past the Jet and Shadow Lakes, the trail continues a gentle descent, through timber and across open meadows. As you pass the nose of a north–south ridge, you begin a climb taking you to Crater Lake. It sits on a shelf below Blair Mountain. From here, the trail ascends, using switchbacks to make the climb easier until you reach the top of the limestone wall. The Crater Lake Trailhead is one-half mile west, down the open slope.

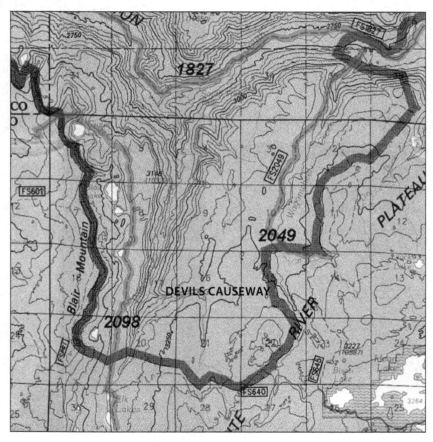

TRAILHEAD 2049 AND 2098

APPENDIX

WILDERNESS LODGES AND OUTFITTERS

Adams Lodge Outfitters
6389 County Road 4, PO Box 1377
Meeker, CO 81641
(970) 878-4312
adamslodgeoutfitters.com

Ute Lodge
393 County Road 75
Meeker, CO 81641
(970) 878-4669
utelodge.com

Ripple Creek Lodge
39020 County Road 8
Meeker, CO 81641
(970) 878-4725
ripplecreeklodge.com

Trappers Lake Lodge & Resort
7700 Trappers Lake Road
Meeker, CO 81641
(970) 878-3336 or (970) 878-5288
trapperslake.com

Budge's Flattops Wilderness Lodge
(901) 466-2265
budges@budgeslodge.com
budgeslodge.com

ADDITIONAL RESOURCES

Colorado Fishing Network
Fishing Information, Fly Shops, Guides
www.coloradofishing.net

Colorado Parks and Wildlife
6060 Broadway
Denver, CO
(303) 291-7227
www. wildlife.state.co.us

0088 Wildlife Way
Glenwood Springs, CO 81601
(970) 947-2920

US Forest Service / Rocky Mountain Region
740 Simms St.
Golden, CO 80401
(303) 275-5350
National Forest Maps:
www.fs.fed.us

Bureau of Land Management Colorado State Office
2850 Youngfield St.
Lakewood, CO 80215
(303) 239-3600
Colorado Surface Ownership Maps: www.blm.gov/co

US Geological Survey Real Time Colorado Stream Flows
waterdata.usgs.gov/co

Colorado Division of Water Resources
www.dwr.state.co.us/SurfaceWater

FEDERAL AGENCIES

US Forest Service / Rocky Mountain Regional Office
740 Simms St.
Golden, CO 80401
(303) 275-5350

White River National Forest
Forest Supervisor
Old Federal Building
PO Box 848
Glenwood Springs, CO 81601
(970) 945-2521

Blanco Ranger District (White River National Forest)
220 East Market St.
Meeker, CO 81641
(970) 878-4039

Eagle Ranger District (White River National Forest)
125 West 5th St.
PO Box 720
Eagle, CO 81631
(970) 328-6388

Rifle Ranger District (White River National Forest)
0094 County Road 244
Rifle, CO 81650
(970) 625-2371

Yampa Ranger District (Routt National Forest) / Routt National Forest
300 Roselawn Ave.
PO Box 7
Yampa, CO 80483
(970) 638-4516

EMERGENCY SERVICES

All Emergencies 911

Eagle County
Vail Valley Medical Center
181 W. Meadow Drive
Vail, CO 81658
(970) 476-2451

Eagle County Sheriff
0885 E. Chambers Ave.
Eagle, CO 81631
(970) 328-8500

Garfield County
Valley View Hospital
1906 Blake Ave.
Glenwood Springs, CO 81601
(970) 945-6535

Clagett Memorial Hospital
701 E. 5th St.
Rifle, CO 81650
(970) 625-1510

Garfield County Sheriff
107 8th St.
Glenwood Springs, CO 81601
(970) 945-0453

Colorado Parks and Wildlife
0088 Wildlife Way
Glenwood Springs, CO 81601
(970) 947-2920

Rio Blanco County
Pioneers Hospital
345 Cleveland St.
Meeker, CO 81641
(970) 878-5047

Rio Blanco County Sheriff
Meeker County Courthouse
555 Main Street
Meeker, CO 81641
(970) 878-9620

Colorado Parks and Wildlife
73485 State Highway 64
Meeker, CO 81641
(970) 878-6090

Moffat County
The Memorial Hospital
785 Russell St.
Craig, CO 81625
(970) 824-9411

Colorado State Patrol
District 4 Commander
554 Jurassic Court
Fruita, CO 81521
(970) 858-2250

Moffat County Sheriff
911

Routt County
Routt Memorial Hospital
80 Park Ave.
Steamboat Springs, CO 80487
(970) 879-1322

Colorado State Patrol
Craig Regional
   Communication Center
800 West 1st Street, Suite 500
Craig, CO 81625
(970) 824-6501
(970) 826-4891 Fax

Routt County Sheriff 911

State
Poison Control
1 (800) 222-1222

Colorado Parks and Wildlife
Headquarters
6060 Broadway
Denver, CO 80216
(303) 297-1192

Northwest Region
711 Independent Ave.
Grand Junction, CO 81505
(970) 255-6100

INDEX

Page locators in *italics* indicate maps and photographs.

acute mountain sickness (AMS), 35–37, 39
Adams Lodge Outfitters, 215
alpine fir, 56
altitude sickness, 35–39
the Amphitheatre, 115, 117, 122
Anderson Lake, 116
Anderson Reservoir Trail, 129–30, *136*
aspen groves, 22
Auerbach, Paul S., 38

Bailey Lake, 53, 56
Bailey Lakes, 176, 177
Bailey Lakes Trail 1859, 177–78
Baldy Creek, 145
basalt flows, 15–16
Bear River, 171
Bear River Trail 1120, 170–72
bears, 19, 31
beaver ponds, 20, 85, 126, 147, 210
Bessies Falls, 105
bicycles, Duck Lake Trail 2261, 109
Big Fish Creek, 107, *131*
Big Fish Fire, 33, 104, *105*, *108*
Big Fish Lake, 51, 105–6
Big Fish Trail 1819, 103–6, *105*, *131*
bighorn sheep, 19
Big Marvine Peak, 90–91, 138, 169
Big Marvine Peak Trail 1822.2A, 90–91
Big Park, 92
Big Park Creek, 94
Big Ridge, 89, 91–92, 95
Big Ridge Cutoff Trail 1820.1A, 95–96
Big Ridge Trail 182091-3, *93*, *99*
Big Ridge Trail junction, 93, 102
Big Spring, 193, 195
birds, 20–21

Bison Lake, 212
Black Mandall Lake, 162, 163
Black Mountain Creek, 153
Black Mountain Trail 1117, 152–53
Blair Lake, 211, 213
Blair Lake Trail 2098, 211–14, *214*
Blair Mountain, 213
Blue Mountain Creek, 143–44, 145
boots, 42
Boulder Lake, 105, 107
Boulder Lake Trail 2262, 106–7
Broken Rib Spring, 204
Buck Lake, 193
Budges Flattops Wilderness Lodge, 60, 62, 68, 71, 209, 211
Buford, 25, 45, 212–13
Bureau of Land Management, Colorado State Office, 216
Burns, 179, 180
Burns Post Office, 179

Campbell Creek, 80
camping and hiking: altitude sickness, 35–39; boots, 42; campsite selection, 51, 61, *61*, 64, 86, *86*, 92, 105–6, 110–11, *174*; clothing, 41; commonsense practices, 30–35; hiking staffs, 41; regulations, 27–30; trail descriptions overview, 42–43; trail selection, 43–44
Carhart, Arthur, 18, 122
Carhart Trail 1815, 121–22
Causeway Lake, 146–47, 165
chickadees, 20
Chief Colorow, 14
Chief Douglas, 13
Chinese Wall, 16, 112, 117, 120–21, 122, 125, 126, 127
Chinese Wall Trail 1803, 137–40
chipmunks, 19, 30–31

Clam Lake, 49, 54, 55
climate, 22–24
clothing, 41
Coal Creek, 159–60
coal mining, 17
Coffin Lake, 119–20
Cold Springs Creek, 166, 167
Colorado Division of Water
  Resources, 216
Colorado Division of Wildlife, 112–13
Colorado Fishing Network, 216
Colorado Parks and Wildlife (CPW),
  119, 122, 124, 209, 216
Colorado River, 17, 24, 26, 179
Colorado River Road. See Eagle
  County Road 301 (Colorado River
  Road)
commonsense practices: altitude
  sickness, 35–39; camping and
  hiking regulations, 27–30;
  dehydration, 34, 37–38; drinking
  water, 34; forest fires, 33, 33;
  hypothermia, 32; insects, 34;
  lightning, 32–33; livestock, 27, 28,
  34–35; physical conditioning, 37,
  39; snakes, 34; standing dead trees
  and windfall, 34; wild animals,
  30–31
cottontail rabbits, 19
County Road 8. See Forest Road 8
  (County Road 8)
coyotes, 19, 30, 31
Craig, 11, 24, 25
Crater Lake, 211, 213
Crescent Lake, 124, 188, 194

Dead Mexican Gulch, 146, 164–65
Deep Creek, 156
Deep Creek Overlook, 204–5, 205
Deep Lake, 15–16, 152, 204
deer, 18, 19
Deer Lake, 141
Deer Lake Trail 1802, 140–41
Deer Park, 185
dehydration, 34, 37–38
Derby Creek, 141, 174, 184, 185, 194
Derby Junction, 156, 179

Derby Mesa Loop, 156, 179, 185
Derby Peak, 174–75, 181, 182
Devils Causeway, 139, 144, 147–48,
  165, 168–70, 169, 170, 214
Diamox, 38–39
Doe Creek, 62, 71–72, 207
Doe Creek Falls, 72
Doe Creek Trail 2259, 50, 70–72
dogs, 27–28, 163
Dome Peak, 181
Doris Lake, 107
Dotsero, 24
Dotsero Crater, 16–17, 18
drinking water, 34, 174, 193
Duck Lake Trail 2261, 109
Dunkley Flat Tops, 153
Dunkley Pass, 142, 153
dusky (blue) grouse, 21

Eagle County Road 39, 179
Eagle County Road 301 (Colorado
  River Road): area driving directions, 179–80, 196; Eagle County
  Road 39, 179; Flat Tops Wilderness
  access, 25–26; Forest Road 610,
  180; Forest Road 613, 185–86;
  Forest Road 616, 192; Hooper,
  Keener Lakes, 189; Hooper Lake
  Trail 1860, 180–81; Island Lake Trail
  1842, 181–82; Johnny Meyers Lake
  Trail 2067, 198–99; Middle Derby
  Trail 1858, 183–85; Rim Lake Trail
  1856, 201–2; Roberts Trail 2076,
  186–87; Shingle Peak Trail 2042,
  199–201; Solitary Lake Trail 1846,
  182–83; South Derby Trail 1857,
  187–88; South W Mountain Trail
  2060, 194–95; Surprise Lake, 196;
  Turret Creek Trail 1832, 197–98;
  Turret–Crescent Trail 2269, 191–92;
  W Mountain, 190, 203; W Mountain
  Trail 1817, 190, 192–94
Eagle River, 17
East Coal Creek, 159
East Fork Trail 1119, 114–18
East Fork Trail 1119 (Stillwater
  Reservoir Trailhead), 167

East Marvine Trail 1822, 46, 87–90, *88*
east trails maps, *8*, *164*, *172*
East Williams Fork, 144, 145–46, 167
Edge Lake, 175–76, 177
Edge Lake Trail, 176–77
Edgeview trail, 57
electrical storms, 32–33
electrolytes, 38
elk, 18, *69*, 70, 72, 107, 129, 150
Emerald Lake fire, 185
emergency services, 218–19
Engelmann spruce, 56
erosion, 14, 15, 116–17, 169–70

false Solomon's seal, 128–29
Fawn Creek, 67
Fawn Creek Trail 1838, 66–68, *67*
federal agencies, 217
Field Guide to Wilderness Medicine (Auerbach), 38
fireweed, *29*, 108
fishing: Blue Mountain Creek, 143–44; Coffin Lake, 119–20; Doe Creek, 71; Gwendolyn Lake, 106; Island Lakes, 188; Lost Lakes, 148; Mandall Lakes, 161–62; Marvine Creek, 84; McGinnis Lake, 127; Mirror Lake, 102; Sable Lake, 92; Shamrock Lake, 101–2; Skinny Fish Lake, 127; Surprise Lake, 123; Trappers Lake, 112–13; Ute Creek, 80
Flat Top Mountain, *11*, 169, 174
Flat Tops Wilderness Area overview: access, 17–18, 24–26; activities, 12–13; climate, 22–24; fauna, 18–21, *19*, *20*; Flat Top Mountain, *11*; geology and formation of, 11–12, 14–17, *16*; glaciation of, 16, *16*; gold mining, 17; history of, 13–14; maps for, 40–42; minerals, 17; preservation of, 18; trail descriptions, 42–44; vegetation, 21–22; visitors to, 11, 12–13. *See also* maps
float tube hatch, *114*
Florence Lake, 110–11
forest fires, *29*, 33, *33*

Forest Road 8 (County Road 8): Chinese Wall Trail 1803, 137–40; Deer Lake Trail 1802, 140–41
Forest Road 16: area driving directions, 142; Black Mountain Trail 1117, 152–53; East Fork Trail 1119, 114–18; Lost Lakes Trail 1116, 148–51, *149*, *154*; Mandall Lakes, *155*; Transfer Trail 1172, 143–44; West Lost Lake Trail 1103, 151–52
Forest Road 205 (Trappers Lake Road): Anderson Reservoir Trail, 129–30, *136*; Big Fish Trail 1819, 103–6, *105*, *131*; Boulder Lake Trail 2262, 106–7; Carhart Trail 1815, 121–22; Duck Lake Trail 2261, 109; Himes Peak Trail 1877, 109–14, *111*, *112–14*; Island Lakes, *133*; Lake of the Woods Trail 2263, 107–8, *108*; Little Trappers Lake, *134*; Mirror Lake Trail 1821, 100–103, *102*; Picket Pin-Lily Pond Trail 1811, 127–29; Skinny Fish Lake, *135*; Skinny Fish Trail 1813, 125–27; Stillwater Trail 1814, 118–21; Surprise Lake Trail (abandoned), 123; Trappers Lake Trail 1816, 123–25, *132*; Wall Lake Trail 1818, 115–18, *117*, *118*
Forest Road 244, 25
Forest Road 600: access to Flat Tops Wilderness, 26; area driving directions, 204; Blair Lake Trail 2098, 211–14, *214*; Deep Creek Overlook, 204–5, *205*; Trailhead 2049 and 2098, *214*; Trappers Lake Trail 1816, 205–9, *208*; Wagon-wheel Creek Trail 2049, 209–11, *214*
Forest Road 610, 180
Forest Road 613, 185–86
Forest Road 616, 192
Fowler Creek, 55–56, 57
Fowler Creek Trail 2256, 55–56
Fowler Rim Trail 2257, 56–57
Fraser Creek, 122

Garfield County line, 196
gates and fences, 60, 87, 101

geology, 11–12, 14–17, *16*
glaciation, 16, *16*, 89, 112, 168
Glenwood Canyon, 17
Glenwood Springs, 24, 26
gold deposits, 17
golden eagles, 21
Grand Hogback, 12, 24
Grand Junction, 11, 24
gray jays, 20
grouse, dusky (blue) grouse, 21
Guthrie Lake, 89
Gwendolyn Lake, 106

HACE (high altitude cerebral edema), 35–37
HAPE (high altitude pulmonary edema), 35–37
Heart Lake, 204, 212
hiking. *See* camping and hiking
hiking staffs, 41
Hill Creek Trail 2255, 53–54, *54*, 55, 57
Himes Peak, 104–5, 106, 110
Himes Peak Campground, 51, 100, 104, 111
Himes Peak Trail 1877, 109–14, *111*, *112–14*
Hooper Lake, 175, *178*, *189*
Hooper Lake Trail 1860, 180–81
Horseshoe Lake, 70
House Creek, 81
hummingbirds, 20
hunting, 18, 23, 29–30
hypothermia, 32

Indian Camp Pass, 118, 125, 202, 204
Indian Camp Trailhead, 125
Indian Lake, 206
insects, 34, 116
Interstate 70 access to Flat Tops Wilderness, 24
Island Lake, 176, 188
Island Lakes, 194
Island Lake Trail 1842, *133*, 181–82

Jet Lake, 213
Johnny Meyers Lake, 198, 199

Johnny Meyers Lake Trail 2067, 198–99
Johnson Lake, 89, 95
Johnson, Lyndon, 18
Johnson Park, 49

Keener Lake, 175, *178*, *189*
Klines Folly Campground, 212
Kremmling, 25

Lake Avery Dam, 46
Lake of the Woods Trail 2263, 107–8, *108*
lichens, 86
lightning, 32–33
Lily Pond Park, 129
Little Causeway Lake, 165
Little Flat Tops, 159
Little Marvine Peaks, 88, *88*, 90, 138, 169
Little Trappers Lake, 119, 120, *134*
livestock, 27, 28, 34–35
Long Expedition, 13
Long Lake, 150
Lost Creek Guard Station, 25, 46
Lost Lake Fire, 104
Lost Lakes Peaks, 137, 138, 139, 149–50, *149*, 152, 169
Lost Lakes Trail 1116, 148–51, *149*, *154*
Lost Solar Creek, 59, 61, 64, 70
Lost Solar Park, 50, 60, 65, 70
Lost Solar Trail 1828, 63–65
Lower Marvine Lake, 85–86
Lower Smith Lake, 166

Mackinaw Lake, 124, 188, 194
Maggies Nipple, 159
mallards, 21
Mandall Creek, 162
Mandall Lakes, 161–63, *166*
Mandall Lakes Trail 1121, *155*, 161–65, *166*
Mandall Pass, 139, 146, 162, 163–65
maps: Anderson Reservoir, *136*; area map, *6–7*; Big Fish Creek, *131*; Big Ridge, *99*; Devils Causeway, *170*;

east trails, *8*, *172*; Hooper, Keener Lakes, *178*, *189*; Island Lakes, *133*; Little Trappers Lake, *134*; Lost Lakes, *154*; Mandall Lakes, *155*, *166*; maps for the Flat Tops, 40–42; Marvine Lakes, *98*; Oyster Lake Trail 1825, *73–74*; Papoose Basin, *97*; Skinny Fish Lake, *135*; South Fork White River, *75*; Surprise Lake, *196*; Trail 1816, *208*; trail descriptions overview, 42–43; Trailhead 2049 and 2098, *214*; Trappers Lake, *132*; Upper South Fork White River, *76*; USGS quads and NGS maps, 40–41; west trails, *9*; White River National Forest map, 40, 43; W Mountain, *190*, *203*

Maroon Bells-Snowmass Wilderness Area, 174

Marvine Campground, 81

Marvine Creek, 83–84

Marvine Creek Campground, 81–82

Marvine Lakes, 50, 78

Marvine Lakes map, *100*

Marvine Trail 1823, 82–87, *84*

Mary Loch Lake, 89

McCoy, 26

McGinnis Lake, 126, 127

McMillan Lake, 184

the Meadows, 58, 59, 61, 62, 64, 67, *67*

meat poles, 29–30

Medicine for the Outdoors (Auerbach), 38

Meeker, 24, 25, 45

Meeker, Nathan, 13

mice, 19

Middle Derby Trail 1858, 183–85

Mill Creek, 14

Mirror Lake, 101, 102–3

Mirror Lake Trail, 93

Mirror Lake Trail 1821, 100–103, *102*

moose, *20*, 21

Mosquito Lake, 170, 171

mountain building processes, 14–15

mountain lions, 19, 31

Mount Kilauea, 15

Mud Lake, 182

Mud Mandall Lake, 163

Muskrat Lake, 182

muskrats, 20

National Geographic Society (NGS) maps, 40

Native Americans, 13–14

New Castle, 24

New Castle-Buford Road, 25

Nichols Creek, 62, 68, 69

Nichols Creek Trail 1830, 68–70

Nimerick Point, 78

North Derby Trail 1122 and Hooper Lake Trail 1860, 172–76, *174*

North Fork Campground, 46

North Fork of the White River County Roads 8 and 12: Big Marvine Peak Trail 1822.2A, 90–91; Big Ridge, *99*; Big Ridge Cutoff Trail 1820.1A, 95–96; Big Ridge Trail 182091-3, *93*; East Marvine Trail 1822, 46, 87–90, *88*; Marvine Lakes, *98*; Marvine Trail 1823, 82–87, *84*; Papoose Basin, *97*; Papoose Creek Trail 2248, 45, 49, 77–78, *78*; Ute Creek Trail 1824, 45, 79–81, *80*; West Marvine Creek Trail 1868 (abandoned), 81–82; Wild Cow Park Trail 1820.1B, 93–95

North Fork White River, 101, 105, *112*

Oak Creek, 24, 25

Orno Peak, 159–61, 163

outfitters, wilderness lodges and outfitters, 215

Outlet Trailhead, 119

Oyster Lake, 49–50, 81

Oyster Lake Trail 1825, 45, 46, 47–51, *48*, *73–74*

Pagoda Peak, 139

Pangea, 14

Papoose Basin, 77, 78

Papoose Basin map, *97*

Papoose Creek, 77, 78

Papoose Creek Trail 2248, 45, 49, 77–78, *78*

Paradise Creek, 103
Park Creek, 60, 66, 69
Park Creek Trail 1829, 65–66
Parvin Lake, 124, 208
Patterson Creek, 211
Peltier Lake, 49, 52–53
Peltier Lake Trail 1826, 51–53
peregrine falcons, 21
Petterson, Eric, 164–65
Phippsburg, 24, 25, 142, 157
physical conditioning, 37, 39
Picket Pin Creek, 128
Picket Pin-Lily Pond Trail 1811, 127–29
Pike Expedition, 13
pine squirrels, 19
plate tectonics, 14–15
porcupines, 19
pothole lakes, 49, 69–70, 80, 116, 188
precipitation, 22–23
private property, 40, 48, 59–60, 61,
    64, 81, 93, 95, 101, 180, 197
Pyramid Guard Station, 142, 144–45,
    165
Pyramid Peak, 145–46, 153, 157

Rabbit Ears Pass, 25
rabbits, 19
Rainbow Lake, 89, 171
raptors, 20–21
Rat Mountain, 84
ravens, 20
red columbines, 108, 120
red-tailed hawks, 20–21
regulations: camping and hiking,
    27–30; dogs, 27–28; livestock, 28;
    trailhead registration, 28–29, 123
Retaining Pond, 150, 151
Rifle, 12, 24
Rifle Gap Reservoir, 12
Rim Lake, 66, 68, 125, 200, 207
Rim Lake Trail 1856, 201–2
Rio Blanco County Road 8: access to
    Flat Tops Wilderness, 25; area
    driving directions, 45–47; Buford,
    45; Doe Creek Trail 2259, 70–72;
    Fawn Creek Trail 1838, 66–68, 67;
    Fowler Creek Trail 2256, 55–56;

Fowler Rim Trail 2257, 56–57; Hill
    Creek Trail 2255, 53–54, 54; Lost
    Solar Trail 1828, 63–65; Meeker, 45;
    Nichols Creek Trail 1830, 68–70;
    Oyster Lake Trail 1825, 45, 46,
    47–51, 48, 73–74; Park Creek Trail
    1829, 65–66; Peltier Lake Trail 1826,
    51–53; South Fork Trail 1827, 45,
    58–62, 59, 61; South Fork Trail 1827
    heading West, 62–63; South Fork
    White River, 75; Upper South Fork
    White River, 76
Rio Blanco Ranch, 101, 102, 103
Ripple Creek, 138
Ripple Creek Lodge, 215
Ripple Creek Overlook, 46, 149
Ripple Creek Pass, 25, 46, 128, 141,
    142, 149
Roberts Trail 2076, 186–87
robins, 20
Round Lake, 146, 147, 150
Routt County line, 142

Sable Lake, 92–93
Sable Point, 92
Sand Creek, 160
Sand Creek Trail 1123, 158–60
Sand Point, 153
Sawtooth Trail 1165, 160–61
sedimentary rocks, 12
Shadow Lake, 211, 213
Shallow Lake, 89
Shamrock Lake, 101–2
Sheep Creek, 195
Sheep Mountain, 181, 185, 187
Shepherd Lake, 66, 68, 125, 206
Sheriff Reservoir, 142, 153
Shingle Lake, 207
Shingle Peak, 62, 124, 191–92, 194,
    197, 198, 207
Shingle Peak Trail 2042, 199–201
ski access, 24
Skillet Lake, 171
Skinny Fish Creek, 126
Skinny Fish Lake, 126–27, 135
Skinny Fish Trail 1813, 125–27
Slide Lake, 84–85

Slide Mandall Lake, 163
Smith Lake, 166
Smith Lake Trail, 165–67
Smith, Tom, 166
snakes, 34
snowfall, 23
snowshoe access, 24
snowshoe hares, 19
Solitary Lake, 182, 183
Solitary Lake Trail 1846, 182–83
songbirds, 20
South Derby Trail 1857, 187–88
South Fork Campground, 47, 63–64
South Fork Trail 1827, 45, 58–63, *59, 61*
South Fork White River, 47, 50, 56,
    58–60, *59, 75*, 117, 207–8
South W Mountain Trail 2060, 194–95
spruce beetles, 21
squirrels, pine squirrels, 19
Stahl, Carl J., 18
standing dead trees and windfall, 34,
    80, 104
Star Lake, 51, 193
State Highway 131: access to Flat Tops
    Wilderness, 25; area driving
    directions, 156–58; Bailey Lakes
    Trail 1859, 177–78; Bear River Trail
    1120, 170–72; Destination:
    Unnamed lake inside the wilder-
    ness, 161; Devils Causeway, 168–70,
    169, 170; East Fork Trail 1119
    (Stillwater Reservoir Trailhead),
    167; east trails, *164, 172*; Edge Lake
    Trail, 176–77; Hooper, Keener
    Lakes, *178*; Mandall Lakes Trail 1121,
    161–65, *166*; North Derby Trail 1122
    and Hooper Lake Trail 1860,
    172–76, *174*; Routt County Road 7,
    158; Sand Creek Trail 1123, 158–60;
    Sawtooth Trail 1165, 160–61; Smith
    Lake Trail, 165–67
Steamboat Springs, 24, 25, 156, 157
Steer Lake, 171
Steller's jays, 20
Stillwater Reservoir, 121, 148, 157, 171,
    177
Stillwater Trail 1814, 118–21

stream crossings, 54, 67, 72, 84–85, 89
stream flows, 216
Stump Park, 176
sunscreen, 41
Supply Basin Campground, 210, 212
Surprise Lake, 123, *196*
Surprise Lake Trail (abandoned), 123
Swede Lake, 48–49
Sweetwater Creek, 125, 202, 206–7
Sweetwater Lake, 192, 196

teal, 21
Thornburgh, Thomas T., 13–14
timber, 21
Timber Mountain, 65, 70
Toponas, 12, 156
Trail 1816 map, *208*
trail descriptions overview, 42–43
Trailhead 2049 and 2098 map, *214*
trailhead registration, 28–29, *163*
trail selection, 43–44
Transfer Trail 1172, 143–44
Trappers Lake, 16, 51, 78, 111–14, *112–
    14*, 115, 116, 119, 122, *132*, 140, 208
Trappers Lake Campground, 107
Trappers Lake Lodge & Resort,
    113–14, 215
Trappers Lake Lodge, 100
Trappers Lake Road. *See* Forest Road
    205 (Trappers Lake Road)
Trappers Lake Trail 1816, 123–25, *132*,
    205–9, *208*
Trappers Peak, 50, 51, 116, *118*
trash, 28, 29
Trout Creek, 161
turkeys, 21
Turret Creek, 192, 197, 198, 200
Turret Creek Meadows, 198
Turret Creek Trail 1832, 197–98
Turret–Crescent Trail 2269, 191–92
Turret Peak, 198
Twin Lakes, 50–51, 90
Twin Mandall Lakes, 163

Unnamed lake inside the wilderness,
    161
Upper Island Lake, 188

Upper Marvine Lake, 86–87
Upper South Fork White River, *76*
US Forest Service, Rocky Mountain Region, 216
US Geological Survey (USGS): quad maps, 40; real time Colorado stream flows, 216
US Highway 40 access to Flat Tops Wilderness, 25
Ute Creek, 49, 50, 79–80
Ute Creek Fire, 80, *80*
Ute Creek Trail 1824, 45, 79–81, *80*
Ute Indians, 13–14
Ute Lodge, 82, 215

Vaughn Lake, 142
volcanism, 15–17
voles, 19–20

Wagonwheel Creek, 210, 211
Wagonwheel Creek Trail 2049, 209–11, *214*
Wall Lake, 51, 78, 116, 117
Wall Lake Trail 1818, 115–18, *117*, *118*
warblers, 20
water, drinking water, 34, 174, 193
waterfalls, *71*, 72, 105
waterfowl, 21
weather and climate, 22–24
West Lost Lake, 152
West Lost Lake Trail 1103, 151–52
West Marvine Creek, 81
West Marvine Creek Trail 1868 (abandoned), 81–82
west trails map, *9*
White River, 68–69, *See also* North Fork of the White River County Roads 8 and 12; South Fork White River
White River Agency, 13
White River deer, *19*
White River National Forest map, 40, 43
White River Uplift, 12
Wilbur Lake, 56, 57
wild animals, 30–31
Wild Cow Park Trail, 92

Wild Cow Park Trail 1820.1B, 93–95
Wilderness Act of 1964, 18, 122
wilderness lodges and outfitters, 215
wildfire: about, 21–22; Big Fish Fire, 33, 104, *105*, *108*; Ute Creek Fire, 80, *80*
wildflowers, 22, 50, 198
wild turkeys, 21
Williams, Bill, 145
W Mountain Trail 1817, *190*, 192–94, *203*
Wolcott, 25, 156, 179
woodpeckers, 20

Yamcola Reservoir, 162
Yampa, 12, 24, 25, 142, 156–57, 179
Yampa River, 17

About the Authors

Since his first visit to the Flat Tops in 1969, **AL MARLOWE** has returned many times. He has backpacked, fished, hunted, camped, and explored the wilderness.

Al lives with his wife, Jean, and their golden retrievers in east Clear Creek County, Colorado. He has a BS in geology and worked several years in the oil industry. In 2000, he established Hidden Lakes Press to publish fishing and hiking guides on CD.

After leaving the oil industry he worked as an outdoor writer. His articles were published in numerous outdoor magazines. In 1994 his first book, *A Hiking and Camping Guide to the Flat Tops Wilderness Area,* was published by Fred Pruett Books in Boulder, Colorado. In 1997 Pruett Publishing in Boulder, Colorado, published his second book, *Fly Fishing the Colorado River: An Angler's Guide.* After establishing Hidden Lakes Press his first guide was *Fly Fishing the Flat Tops.* Subsequent work has included fly fishing guides coauthored by Evergreen angler Karen Christopherson. Their guides, *Fly Fishing the North Platte River, Fly Fishing the Colorado River, Fifty Colorado Tailwaters,* and *Trout on Colorado State Land,* are available at coloradofishing.com.

KAREN RAE CHRISTOPHERSON has been fishing since her childhood in Boulder, Colorado. A geophysicist by education and training, Karen has

traveled extensively throughout the US and across the world, often with her fly rod in tow. Writing has been a passion since school and she feels fortunate to author books about fly fishing as a diversion from the technical world of geosciences. Karen also acts as webmaster for coloradofishing.net and other fishing websites.